To all who read this book, we want to express our complete endorsement, love and support to Barry and his lovely wife Linda, who we have had the pleasure to serve with these last nine plus years in the PROPHETIC ministry of helping G-D's chosen children (the Jewish people) return to Israel. The return of the Jewish people to Israel is the greatest prophetic happening in our lifetime. You will be blessed as Barry takes you through the years of G-D's calling on his life. I pray the words of this book will help you in putting action to the calling G-D has on your life.

Mel & Joanne Hoelzle
Founders/Ezra International

Barry and Linda Wagner are opening new doors and fulfilling prophecy in the Middle-East while hostile clocks are racing to close their avenues of opportunity. *And Still They Come—Israel's "Final Return"* is required reading for those who realize we are living in the last days every day.

William Carr Blood
Retired military and author, Miracles *and* The Final Exodus

Reverend Barry Wagner has written a passionate and persuasive book concerning the very heart of God. He clearly captures God's desire to re-gather the Jewish people back to the land of Israel and the mandate to the church to be involved. I believe equally compelling is his personal faith journey to find the perfect will of God for his life. This book is a must read to every person who has heard the call of God and desires to be one who will say, "Here am I, use me."

Reverend Gary Cristofaro
Senior Pastor, First Assembly of God
Melbourne FL

And Still They Come

Israel's "Final Return"

God's End Time Plan for
Israel, the Jewish People
and the Church

Rev. Barry L. Wagner

Bible prophecy is being fulfilled before our eyes concerning
Israel, the Jewish people and the Church.
How will it all affect you?

And Still They Come
Israel's "Final Return"
by Rev. Barry L. Wagner

Printed in the United States of America.

International Standard Book Number 978-0-615-18557-6

Cover design and typography by Ambassador Productions, Gainesville, Florida

This Book Is Gratefully Dedicated To

The many thousands of Jewish people
who have so richly blessed my life
over these past nine years as we have
labored in the *aliyah*.

"Thank You So Very Much For Your Love"

*"I will bless those who bless you,
whoever curses you I will curse;
And all peoples on earth
will be blessed through you."*
Genesis 12:3 NIV

With A Heart Full Of Appreciation

My feeble words can never fully express my heart-felt appreciation to Linda—my wife, my constant companion and the light of my life—for her unwavering support in everything that God has ever called us to do for the Kingdom. She has stood faithfully by my side through the good times and the not-so-good times. Her deep love for God, for His plans and purposes for our lives, her love for our children, our grandchildren and her husband has been a role-model for thousands of wives and mothers over these past forty-two years. She is truly my gift from God.

"A wife of noble character who can find? She is worth far more than rubies. Her husband has full confidence in her and lacks nothing of value."
Proverbs 31:10-11

Table of Contents

Part 3   God's Plan For the Jews and the Church

Foreword

When I was finally convinced that it was God leading me to write this book on the subject of the "Final Return" of the Jewish people to their "Promised Land," I thought at first I would write only of this great prophetic event. It was only a short time later that I knew God was directing me to develop this book with a two fold purpose.

It was to be a book to help the Body of Christ particularly and people of all faiths in general to understand what God is doing prophetically with the Nation of Israel and the Jewish people in these last days.

It was also to be a book of ministry. My prayer is that by sharing many things from my own past as to how God called, prepared and eventually sent me forth into a new calling, it will help those who are struggling with their own callings.

Everywhere I travel I meet many sincere Christian brothers and sisters who are struggling with being able to step out in faith or being able to totally trust God for their every need. A new thing is happening in their lives which they don't fully understand. Often it is God who has placed them on the fast track to a complete breaking, sanctifying, and bringing them to a point of being able to trust fully in His provision.

All of this is a time of preparation for what God has for them in the not-too-distant future. All of it is a very necessary process that God needs to take them through to make them better fit for the Master's use.

Many know that God is placing a new calling on their lives but it has not been fully revealed, and it is so terribly frustrating. It is my hope that the first eight chapters of this book will teach, encourage, and bring some clarity to what they may be experiencing in this process.

Still others for the first time in their Christian walk are finding that somehow and for some reason they now have a deep love in their heart for the Jewish people and the land of Israel. They may have no idea where it came from or why they are feeling this way.

Suddenly they have a real desire to learn as much about the rich Hebraic foundation of the Christian faith as they possibly can, but they don't understand why they feel such a need.

Hopefully, tucked between the pages of this book they will find the answers they are so desperately seeking. Perhaps you are one of those people. If you are, I would like to share this thought with you even before you begin your reading. What you are experiencing in your life right now—the testing, the trials, the uncertainty—is of great value to you and your future calling.

So be encouraged. Take heart; rest in the Lord and simply *"Be still and know that I am God"* (Psalm 46:10a).

One last note: while I do draw from my own personal experiences in the first eight chapters of this book, I do so to help others understand what God is doing in *their* lives, but those chapters are not about the man Barry Wagner; they ARE about an all-knowing, all-loving, all-caring, all-compassionate God who is full of mercy and grace. Our God who loves each of us so much He is willing to allow trials and tests to come into our lives for the purpose of maturing us and bringing us to that place where He can use us for His greatest good and glory.

*"Consider it pure joy, my brothers, whenever you face **trials** of many kinds, because you know that the **testing** of your faith develops perseverance. Perseverance must finish its' work so that you may be mature and complete, not lacking anything"* (James 1:2-4 NIV, emphasis mine).

Introduction

There is so much bad news bombarding us every day of our lives that it becomes easy to just wish it would all go away. Good news is quite rare in these days we find ourselves living, so we must seek it out wherever it may be found.

One of the greatest pieces of good news we could ever hope to find is found in the writings of the Jewish prophets of old—Isaiah, Jeremiah, Amos, Daniel, Ezekiel as well as many of the other prophets. They all wrote of a day, just prior to the return of Messiah, when God would gather His Chosen People from the four corners of the earth. The prophets wrote of this great event when the Jewish people would return to Israel from all the nations over two-thousand, seven hundred years ago.

Jeremiah spoke of it this way: *"However, the days are coming," declares the Lord, "when men will no longer say, 'As surely as the Lord lives, who brought the Israelites up out of Egypt,' but they will say, 'As surely as the Lord lives, who brought the Israelites up out of the land of the north, (Russia), and out of all the countries where He had banished them.' For I will restore them to the land I gave their forefathers"* (Jeremiah 16:14-15).

I believe we are living in the most exciting days that we could ever hope to live in. Today is that prophetic season to which the prophets were referring. The prophetic season when the Jewish people would make *aliyah* (immigrate) from every nation of the earth and return to their "Promised Land." Jeremiah tells us that this exodus would be so large it would eventually overshadow the exodus of the Israelites from Egypt.

Since the walls of Communism fell allowing the Jews of the former Soviet Union countries to leave freely, over one and a half million have fled those countries and are now at home in Israel.

Ezra International has been on the cutting edge since 1995 assisting over sixty-five thousand Jewish people of the FSU (former Soviet Union) countries and Latin America in their return to their homeland.

Ezra International is a non-profit, non-denominational Christian organization of which I have been blessed to serve as vice president for nearly ten years. (More about the work, the ministry, and the calling of Ezra later in this book).

With the many wars the Israelis have had to fight after being invaded time after time by their Arab neighbors; with the years of having to live in fear of chemical warfare, needing to have a sealed room in their home and each family member being fitted for their own gas mask; and dodging incoming rockets, one would think that Israel is not the most likely place to which Jews would have a desire to return. But that is all in the natural. Let us be careful not to forget about the spiritual side of this great world event.

This massive return from the nations of the Jewish people is called *aliyah*. The word *aliyah* is a Hebrew word that means literally "to go up," for example, "to go up to Jerusalem."

As I travel around the world speaking in churches and conferences, appearing on television and radio programs, I am constantly asked, *"Barry, are the Jewish people still going up to Israel and Jerusalem?"*

That question is what has prompted the writing of this book. I am so pleased to use this opportunity to answer that question with a resounding YES; they are still coming home!

After the many wars, after all the falling rockets, after the many nights and days in their sealed rooms and bomb shelters, I can honestly say, *"And Still They Come. And Still They Come. And Still They Come."*

Why do they continue to come? What is motivating these precious people of God to leave the countries of their birth and move to a new land—a land completely foreign to them, a different culture, a new language and the unknown? What drives them? What pulls them? Why do they do it?

I will do my very best to answer these sobering questions and many others in the pages of this book—*And Still They Come—Israel's "Final Return."*

Part 1

Time of Preparation

Chapter One

God's Call to Full-time Ministry

"For God's gifts and His call are irrevocable."
Romans 11:29

God speaks to those who diligently seek Him in many different ways. To some He speaks in an audible voice; to others He speaks through friends, a caring pastor or even a total stranger, who many times are not even aware that God is using them to reach the heart of the one seeking after Him. So it was during the eighteen-month period of time that God was calling me to the ministry. My family and I had become involved in a large church in Lakeland, Florida, and God went to work on me immediately. Shortly after my salvation experience I began to feel in my spirit that He was preparing me for something in the not-so-distant future.

I had no objections to becoming a pastor, but even as a baby Christian I knew that the only way it would work out was for it to be God's perfect will for my life and not just my personal desire. So I did the only thing I knew to do. I prayed, and I prayed, and I prayed. I cried out to God from the very depths of my being. I prayed, "Oh God, if it is your *perfect* will for me to be a pastor, please give me a sign."

I am so thankful that we serve a God who is full of patience and grace. I really didn't make it easy on Him before

1

I finally gave in. Once again it wasn't because I didn't want to become a pastor. In fact it was just the opposite. I *did* want to be a pastor but *only* if it was His perfect will for my life. For eighteen months I asked for one sign after another, and they came. But just to make certain, I would ask for another sign, and when it came I would ask for another, and another. Sign after sign was given, and still I did not budge. I just had to know for certain.

During this time of God calling me to ministry, my mother-in-law Gertrude was in an Akron, Ohio hospital dying of cancer. She was scheduled for serious surgery, so Linda and I decided to fly to Akron to be with her. I remember praying on the plane not only for my mother-in-law to be healed, but once again, I prayed that God would give me a sign so I would know for certain that becoming a pastor was His perfect will for my life.

While Gertrude was in surgery, Linda and I went to the coffee shop to have a cup of coffee and to wait it out. While I was going through the serving line for the coffee Linda took a table just beyond the cashier. When I approached the cashier I recognized her as one of my high school classmates that I had graduated with nine years earlier from a neighboring town there in Ohio. I asked her, "You're Phyllis Butterbaugh aren't you?"

She answered, "Well, I was, but I am married now, and my last name has changed."

I could tell that she was somewhat embarrassed because she didn't recognize me. So I introduced myself. I said, "Phyllis, I'm Barry Wagner." Now she really was embarrassed for not recognizing me since we were friends during our high school days.

The next thing she said was, "What are you doing these days?" to which I responded, "I live in Florida, and I would never think of moving back to Ohio." That is the only thing I said to her.

Now remember it was only about two hours earlier that I had asked God for another sign if He truly wanted me to become a pastor. The next words that came out of her mouth were these, *"Barry, are you a minister?"* I could not believe what I had just heard. Here was a girl I had not seen in over nine years. I was living with my family almost a thousand miles from her, and all I said to her was, "I live in Florida, and I would never think of moving back to Ohio," and she says, "Barry, are you a minister?"

I said, "Phyllis, why would you ask such a thing?" Her response was simply, "I don't know, you just sound like one." Wow, I looked at Linda whom I knew had overheard this very strange conversation from where she was sitting. When I sat down at the table with her I said, "Linda, how much plainer does it need to be?"

Here was a lovely young lady who God used to speak to me in a way that finalized my call to the ministry after eighteen long months, and she had no idea whatsoever that God was using her to reach me. To this day I have no idea if Phyllis is even a Christian or not, but God used her to change a life for eternity. My friends, God speaks many times to us through other individuals, some may not even be believers. We just need to hear His voice when He speaks.

That unforeseen experience was used by God to finalize His call on my life. Linda's mother eventually lost her battle with cancer and passed away a few months later, which changed her life for all eternity, but God also used that time to change our lives forever as well.

Just a few months later we would quit our jobs, sell our home and move from Florida to Mt. Vernon, Ohio, where I would attend Mt. Vernon Nazarene College in preparation for full-time ministry.

After leaving college we settled into our first church where I assumed the position of senior pastor. Our first assignment took us to Lake Mary, Florida, where we would serve the Lake Mary Church of the Nazarene.

After our appointed time of ministry at the Lake Mary church ended, God used us over the next twenty-five years as we served churches in Florida and Virginia until His appointed time for our spiritual awakening as it pertains to Israel and the Jewish people would begin.

Chapter Two

The Spiritual Awakening

*"I did not receive it from any man, nor was I taught it;
rather, I received it by revelation from Jesus Christ."*
Galatians 1:12

Thank God for the many spiritual awakenings we receive from the Spirit of God throughout our Christian journey. It is these spiritual awakenings or revelations from God that He uses to move us to the next important level of our spiritual growth and maturity. Without continuing spiritual growth, new understanding, and new revelation taking place in our lives, our Christian walk would become stagnant, and we would remain spiritual infants. It would be impossible for God to use any of us to our greatest potential, and we would miss out on the many blessings that He has laid up for us, not only in heaven, but in this life as well. It is extremely vital that God has mature, fully grown, strong, healthy, willing and obedient soldiers in His spiritual army to accomplish His complete and perfect will in this life.

In every church I speak in around the world I always ask the congregations, "How many of you love to receive new revelation from God?" Almost every hand flies high into the air. And then I say, "Be careful about asking

God for revelation because with every revelation comes responsibility." You see, God doesn't give us new revelation and spiritual understanding just for the sake of it. God doesn't work that way. He gives us new revelation so we can use it for His plans, His purposes and His glory, and it always involves responsibility.

I firmly believe that one of the most important revelations and spiritual awakenings that God wants us all to experience is our relationship with the Jewish people, the land of Israel and how it all pertains to the Church and each of us in these last days that we are presently living in.

Concerning our relationship with the Jewish people, this is what I tell congregations and conferences wherever I speak: "I have found over the past nine years since becoming involved in the *aliyah* that God is miraculously dropping a deep love into the hearts of millions of Christians around the world for the Jewish people. Many of you know exactly what I'm talking about because it has happened to you. You don't know why, but suddenly you have a very real and an extremely deep love in your heart for Jewish people and the land of Israel. Well, if that is you, there are two things I want you to know about what has happened to you. First of all, that deep love you have for the Jewish people man did not put it into your heart. In fact, man is incapable of putting that love in your heart for His people. It was the Holy Spirit of God who put that love in your heart for them. And secondly, God didn't put that love in your heart just for the sake of putting it there. He has done it for such a time as this."

God is raising up a mighty army of millions of Christian believers from every nation, from every tongue, from every walk of life, every denomination, every color of skin—men, women, teenagers, and even children—to stand with the Jewish people, to love them unconditionally, and to help them in their "Final Return" to their "Promised Land" in this last wonderful prophetic season.

My dear Christian friend, perhaps you have not experienced this wonderful thing that God is doing in the hearts of so many believers around the world—how He is dropping this deep abiding love into their hearts for the Jewish people and the land of Israel. Please hear me; no, don't hear me, but hear the voice of the Holy Spirit. God wants to do this marvelous miracle in your life as well. Today, you too can experience this same love in your life that millions of other Christian brothers and sisters have already experienced. That miracle is only a short prayer away. If it is truly your desire to love His chosen people with the same love God has for them, I will ask you to pray a simple prayer at the close of this book which will change your life forever as it has done for me, Linda, and millions of others the world over. You will never be sorry for praying such a life-transforming prayer, I can assure you.

After several years of full-time ministry as a pastor, I felt an overwhelming desire to visit the land of Israel. I had never had the opportunity to make such a spiritual journey. It seemed that if I had the time to go, I didn't have the financial resources, and if I had the financial resources (which was almost never), I didn't have the time. *But God had a plan!*

It was in 1984 that He called me from the pulpit ministry to a Christian organization called Educational Opportunities located in Lakeland, Florida. This organization had become one of the largest Christian tour companies in the United States taking Christian pilgrims to the Holy Land. I was hired by E.O. to fill the position of "Director of Marketing." Since I had never been to Israel, Dr. James Ridgeway, the founder and president of E.O. said, "Barry, if you are going to be marketing our travel programs to Israel, you need to go see for yourself what we are offering."

At that time I didn't even have a passport, so Dr. Ridgeway told me to catch a flight to Miami and walk my passport application through the passport office. I caught a flight for Miami the very next day and began the process at the passport office. Spending the night sleeping in the back seat of my rental car in the parking garage of the Miami airport I was determined to leave Miami with passport in hand. The following day I returned to the passport office and was handed my completed passport.

Within the next few days I found myself on board a Boeing 747 jumbo jet headed for Tel Aviv, Israel. How excited I was to be going to the land I had only read about in the Bible and had preached about for several years. Now, for the first time I would be able to experience the land and walk in the footsteps of Jesus.

After a very long flight of about eleven hours, that great 747 jumbo jet airliner landed at the David Ben-Gurion airport in Tel Aviv. That was in February of 1984, and I can still remember as clearly as if it were only yesterday how the thrill and the anticipation of being in the Holy Land had been building deep within my spirit.

I stepped out of the door of the plane and began to descend the flight of steps that would take me to the tarmac and eventually into the terminal building. Immediately when I had both feet on Israeli soil for the first time, something very strange and quite miraculous happened. I heard the voice of God say to me—not in an audible voice but it was the closest thing to it I had ever experienced—*"Barry, you have been on a sojourn (journey) all your life, and now you have come home."*

I was so powerfully moved upon by the Holy Spirit that I literally fell to my knees right there on the tarmac of David Ben-Gurion airport. I raised my hands toward heaven; I began to shake, tremble and cry uncontrollably as God did a Divine work in my life. My fellow passengers on that flight had to walk around me as I was undergoing spiritual surgery. They must have thought that I had just slipped over the edge and that I was a prime candidate for a mental institution. I'm certain this was a sight those travelers have never forgotten.

I must tell you that I lost something that day, but I gained something as well. God did spiritual surgery on me right there on the tarmac of the David Ben-Gurion airport. He removed from me my Gentile heart, but He gave me something in return. He replaced my Gentile heart with a Jewish heart, and at that moment God put a deep abiding love in my heart for the land of Israel and for the Jewish people. That spiritual surgery has not only changed my life forever, but it has completely transformed my life-long ministry and calling. Since that eventful day in February of 1984, I have been blessed to have made thirty-nine trips to this land that I love so deeply.

In fact, the miracle that took place in my life that day on the tarmac of the Tel Aviv airport has even influenced my funeral arrangements, which have been spelled out in great detail to be used when the time comes that God calls me home.

I have left instructions with my wife, Linda, that I wish for my casket to remain closed during the funeral service. Because I am a Vietnam war veteran having served four years in the United States Air Force, she is to have the bottom half of my casket covered with the American flag from my waist down; and because my heart is so full of love for the land of Israel, it is my desire to have the Israeli flag covering the coffin from my waist over my heart and draping over the head of the coffin.

You see, as Christians we are citizens of two nations. America is our physical homeland, but Israel is our spiritual homeland.

The apostle Paul wrote, *"Remember that at that time you were separate from Christ, excluded from citizenship in Israel ... consequently, you are no longer foreigners and aliens, but fellow citizens with God's people and members of God's household"* (Ephesians 2:12a, 19).

Is it any wonder then why so many Christians feel like they have arrived home every time they step off the airplane and place their feet on Israeli soil no matter how many times they return?

As we now reflect back over the past thirty-three years of full-time ministry we know with no uncertainty that those glorious years were years of preparation for such a time as this. The appointed time to begin our new life-long work was still fourteen years ahead of us. There was still much necessary spiritual preparation to be done. Before God could use us to bless His people in the way He wanted to use us, He first had to do some very serious work in both of our lives. He saw things in our lives that needed to be changed and corrected—things that we were incapable of seeing or even knowing were there

It would take over three years of spiritual surgery to correct the problem. Only by the hands of an extremely skillful Surgeon could the defects be healed. The spiritual surgery that was just ahead of us would begin with serious breaking.

Chapter Three

The Breaking Begins—Ouch!

"Consider it pure joy, my brothers, whenever you face trials of many kinds, because you know that the testing of your faith develops perseverance. Perseverance must finish its work so that you may be mature and complete, not lacking anything."
James 1:2-4

Anyone who has ever had anything to do with horses knows that you can be the proud owner of the most beautiful steed bred from the finest lines, but until that horse is fully broken, there is very little it can be used for. If the owner ever wants his prize stallion to be a riding horse, a show horse, or perhaps a rodeo horse, that animal must be broken and be submissive to its master's every command.

Each one of us as a child of God is much like that thoroughbred stallion. Until we are fully broken we are of little use to our Master. Until we are willing to allow God to have full reign in our lives we will continue to miss our Divine-appointed destiny which was determined before the foundations of the earth were laid. Abba may be pulling the reigns to the left, but we continue going to the right. He may be pulling back on our reigns to stop us, but we continue to move forward. Not until we are fully broken and come to a place of total surrender in our spiritual lives are we fit for the Master's use.

Having served the Church faithfully for many years, I felt that I was fully sanctified, fully broken, and totally submitted to the perfect will of God. However, we must understand that God knows us far better than we know ourselves. He knows our every strength, our every weakness, all of our flaws, all of the warts, and all of our shortcomings. Just when *we* think we would be great candidates for a spiritual Doctorate degree God says, "Not so fast my child; there are still a few things in your life that must first be dealt with before I can fully use you," and He wants to send us back to the first grade to start all over again.

Soon the day would come when Linda and I both would learn what it means to be broken by the loving hand of our Heavenly Father. God's breaking is not like a chef's breaking of an egg as he gently cracks it over the edge of the frying pan ending up with two perfect halves of the egg shell in his hand. That is not God's way of breaking us. We soon discovered that God's way of breaking is extremely thorough.

You see, God takes that same egg (us) in His hand, breaks us over the edge of the frying pan, then drops the two perfect halves of the shell onto the floor and grinds them into a very fine powder with His heal. Ouch!! But oh so desperately needed!

And so it was for Linda and me. We had just left a wonderful pastorate at the First Church of the Nazarene in Woodbridge, Virginia. I had been serving there as a co-pastor and had been enjoying a successful ministry when—at God's appointed time—He made it perfectly clear that I was to resign from my position and seek a different church to serve as Senior Pastor.

I received a call to a church in the Pensacola, Florida area. Linda and I flew to Florida for our interview where we received a unanimous vote to serve as their pastor. Without seeking my helpmate's counsel, I accepted the call. God had many years earlier provided me with the perfect person to seek counsel from, and I foolishly ignored it. Later Linda would share with me that she knew as soon as we pulled onto the church property this was not where God wanted us to be. I would soon pay a dear price for walking in God's "permissive will" instead of waiting for His "perfect will" to be revealed.

I can honestly say that we had a productive ministry at that church, with many people coming to know the Lord, many baptisms, services running at full capacity; and we experienced a great increase in the church finances, yet I was miserable. Unfortunately it was necessary to go to battle with the church board for everything I felt that God was calling us to do. I had to nearly beg for every dime spent on salaries, church improvements, and church programs. Money seemed to be their God, and serious ministry had become a mere side-line event.

The situation there was so bad it nearly destroyed me physically, emotionally, and spiritually. After serving that church for eighteen months, I realized that if I were to survive it would be necessary for me to resign. I gave a thirty-day notice to my board and made preparations for our departure.

On the day that had been scheduled for the move out, I knew that I had made the right decision when I saw that there were more volunteers to help us load the Ryder truck for the move out than there were on the day for the move in. I will never forget the experience I had as I put the truck into first gear and began moving slowly out of the parsonage driveway with my wife and two children following behind in the family sedan. I could physically feel a heaviness lift from my shoulders. It was as if I was driving out from under a dark cloud into the waiting warmth of the Florida sunshine.

That is the only time in the thirty-three years of full-time ministry that I was out of the perfect will of God, and

I knew it. I can tell you from personal experience, it is not a very nice place to be. We must always seek God until His perfect will is revealed to us, then walk boldly into it, knowing that He is going before us.

Linda and I had given all we had. We had poured ourselves out completely to the church and its people until there was nothing left to give. I was completely drained; I was experiencing total burnout. It was then that I made a decision to return to the Orlando area, find a secular job, settle into a local church, and become the best layman a pastor could ever hope to have in his congregation. I would offer myself and my services to this pastor in any capacity. I was willing to even clean toilet bowls if that was required of me. I just wanted to be extremely supportive of the pastor that I would sit under, knowing full well what he must be going through as a pastor for I had walked that walk for many years.

Even though I was returning to the Orlando area to leave the ministry, I was not giving up on God. I was just extremely tired of the unbridled politics in the church, the traditions of man, the necessary battles to try to return the church to its high calling, and the lukewarmness that abounded everywhere. I just felt that time was very short, and I wanted so deeply for my life and my ministry to count for something more than bottle-feeding and burping a fat and happy church that seemed quite satisfied with the status quo day after day, week after week.

Chapter Four

God, What Am I Doing Here?

"Therefore, we do not lose heart. Though outwardly we are wasting away, yet inwardly we are being renewed day by day. For our light and momentary troubles are achieving for us an eternal glory that far out weighs them all."
2 Corinthians 4:16, 17

After finding a house to rent in the small town of Deltona, Florida, about twenty-five miles east of Orlando, God's breaking of our lives began. It seemed that God was about to put us on the fast track to accomplish the much-needed work in our spiritual lives to prepare us for what would come eight years later.

When we arrived in Deltona we had no savings account—only our final pay check from the church we had just left. After paying the first month's rent and the security deposit on the house there was very little of our funds remaining.

Oh, how desperately we both needed to find jobs—or so we thought. I am now convinced that God knows far better than we do what we have need of. Our two teenage sons, Barry and Bryan, had developed a very expensive habit over the years. It's called *eating*. Anyone raising teenagers knows exactly what I am talking about.

For the next six months Linda and I both interviewed day after day for jobs, only to be turned down time after time. Our money was soon gone, and we found ourselves living on our credit cards. Our situation got so bad it became necessary for us to sell furniture from our home just to be able to purchase food for the family.

Eventually Linda secured a job at a doctor's office which at least paid the rent and bought some groceries. I on the other hand continued to be rejected for meaningful employment at every turn. All the while I thought I needed a job, but God knew I needed something far more important and of far greater value. He knew I needed to be fully broken and to come to that place in my spiritual walk that I could and would be totally dependent upon Him and that I would trust Him fully for our every need.

It was an extremely painful lesson but a necessary one in the eyes of God. This painful breaking would last for the next three and one half years, and I can truthfully tell you that it was the most difficult time of our married life. I hope I never have to go through it again, but I also must tell you that it was also the greatest time of my life. Over the next three-and-a-half years I came to know God in ways I had never known Him before. Linda and I experienced more miracles in our lives during that time than we had experienced in all the years we had been walking with Him.

You see, I am a firm believer that we experience far more miracles in our lives when we walk through the wilderness and through the valley of dry bones than we ever do as we stand on the mountain top. For it is in the wilderness, after all, that our human resources are depleted, our physical strength is drained, and we have nothing left to sustain us. It is only then that we have but one person to turn to—the God of Abraham, Isaac and Jacob. Just as He provided manna from heaven, water from the rocks, and birds of the air for the children of Israel as they journeyed forty years in the wilderness, so it is that He wants to provide for us during our trek through the wildernesses of life.

The lesson that God wants each of us to learn is the very same lesson He wanted to teach the Israelites during their exodus from Egypt (Exodus 16-17). God wants us to learn that on every occasion and in every situation of life—no matter what things may look like in the natural—He *can* be trusted and we are to be totally dependent on Him for our every need.

I love the story about the manna from heaven found in Exodus 16:4-7. *Then the Lord said to Moses, "I will rain down bread from heaven for you. The people are to go out each day and gather enough for that day. In this way I will test them and see whether they will follow my instructions. On the sixth day they are to prepare what they bring in, and that is to be twice as much as they gather on the other days."*

Contained in this story is a very important lesson for us all. God told the Israelites to go and gather enough of the manna for only the next day, except on the day before the Sabbath they were to gather enough for each family member to sustain them for two days. Some of the people did not do as they were commanded, and they gathered more than they were permitted to gather only to have it spoil before they could use it. How was God providing for them? Not on a yearly basis, not on a monthly basis, not even on a weekly basis, but on a *daily* basis. The lesson He was trying to teach the Israelites is the same lesson he wants to teach us—that He would provide for their every need and ours, daily, no matter how things may look in the natural. We need only to trust Him.

With the passing of each day, each week, and each month since our return from Pensacola, the frustration over our financial situation only grew deeper and more painful. I had still not secured a meaningful, decent-paying job. I think one of the most difficult things for a husband and a father to experience is not being able to provide for his family. Linda and I had been married since the age of eighteen. She was my high school sweetheart; in fact, she was the only girl I had ever dated. After graduating from high school and after completing my Air Force basic training I returned home on a ten-day leave, and it was then that we were married.

We have been on our own since the age of eighteen, and in all of those years I had never experienced the pain of not being able to provide for my wife and my two sons who would come along five and seven years later. Up until that point in our lives it was "I" that provided for my family, or so I thought. It was through my personal strength, my personal talents, my personal efforts that kept the family going, or so I thought. You see, God wanted to break me of that thinking and teach me that it would be He and only He who would be our provider, especially in the important years to come.

After months of sending out resumes, having gone through interview after interview, and doing everything "I" could do, I finally did the only thing I knew to do. I began working through employment agencies that secured temporary jobs for their clients. One of the first jobs I was sent on at a pay of five dollars per hour was working for a large food distribution operation. I spent the entire day, day after day, working in the trash and garbage removal department where I would shovel thousands of pounds of waste into a huge trash compactor where it would later be hauled off by semi-trucks. Many times during that period I felt much like the prodigal son must have felt like. Here he was, his father was extremely wealthy, his brother was at home enjoying a very comfortable life, and yet he was slopping hogs and eating what they were eating in a foreign land.

After that job ran out I was sent to a Coca-Cola research and development plant—a facility that developed new products for Coke's product line. After several days of doing menial jobs of all types I found myself sitting on a five gallon bucket turned upside down with a water hose in one hand and a large scrub brush in the other. Before me were piles of hundreds of dirty five gallon buckets, and it was *my* job to scrub them clean so they could be reused in the labs to hold experimental liquid products.

So, here I sat, day after day scrubbing out dirty five gallon buckets, wondering what in the world I was doing there. After all, I had spent over twenty years in full-time ministry after my college years. I had always been successful in whatever I did.

In all our years of marriage I never had trouble providing for my family, and NOW I find myself doing a job a ten year old could do. What was happening to me? What was this all about? Why did God have me in such a lowly position? Could He see something in my life that needed fixing—something perhaps that needed to be removed? What was it that was so bad that He had to bring me to this low point in my life? I have learned through this experience and many others that so often God has to bring us to the very bottom before He can move us to the top, to that position, to that place where He desires us to be. It is then, after the breaking, after the spiritual surgery is completed, that He can finally begin to use us in ways we never thought possible.

We would soon come to learn that God wanted to reveal Himself to us as the miracle-working God. The only way we could possibly get through this time of breaking would be due to the many miracles He would perform over the next three-and-a-half years on our behalf.

Chapter Five

Miracles In the Wilderness

*"You are the God who performs miracles;
you display your power among the peoples."*
Psalm 77:14

One of the many miracles that I experienced during this "wilderness experience" involved Pastor Sam Hinn, Benny Hinn's brother. God began setting the stage for this miracle when my family and I began attending Benny's church on Sunday evenings. I had never had the opportunity to meet Sam or even to shake his hand. He had never seen me, and the only way I knew him was by seeing him on the platform each service with his brother, Benny.

One Sunday evening as we were attending the service I noticed a person in the choir whom I had known many years earlier. It was Sharon Peterson who had been my piano player in the very first church that I pastored in Lake Mary, Florida. Her husband Danny served as my music director. After the service that night Linda and I made it a point to find her and Danny to invite them to go out for a time of coffee, dessert, and some much-needed fellowship to renew our acquaintance after so many years.

During our time together that evening I never told Danny and Sharon about the wilderness experience in which we were walking. We simply spoke of those wonderful days we shared together so many years earlier while pastoring our first church. At one point I mentioned to them that I had been involved in deliverance ministry.

During our conversation together Sharon told us that she was the private secretary to the administrator of Benny Hinn's church, Orlando Christian Center. A few days later, while at work she was speaking to Sam Hinn in passing and mentioned that she had been reacquainted with her former pastor and wife. She also mentioned that I had been involved in deliverance ministry, which was of great interest to Sam. He told Sharon that he would like to meet me and to have an opportunity to compare ministry notes, so-to-speak.

The next Wednesday evening I attended the mid-week service at Orlando Christian Center and sat on the third row from the front. After a beautiful time of praise and worship Pastor Benny stood to receive the offering. He had the congregation turn to Psalms 126:5-6 which declares, *"Those who sow in tears will reap with songs of joy. He who goes out weeping, carrying seed to sow, will return with songs of joy carrying sheaves with him."* At that moment I realized that during all the previous years of walking with and serving the Lord, I had never sown in tears. I had always given God His tithes, I had always supported our missionaries, I had always given alms for the needy, but it was always out of our abundance. I had no idea what it meant to sow in tears, that is, until that Wednesday evening. That night I learned a lesson that changed my life forever.

As the offering bags were being passed, I heard the Holy Spirit say to me, *"Barry, give me what you have."* The Lord's voice was so clear it actually startled me.

I said, "But God, you know what I have; it's so little." When I did not move to respond to His voice, He said it again. *"Barry, give me what you have."*

So I did the only thing I could do. I reached into my pocket and there I found four, one dollar bills and loose change that totaled a dollar. That night, as usual, we had no money in a savings account, no money in the checking account. Linda had no money; we had only that five dollars between us and heaven. In total obedience I dropped my last five dollars into the offering bag, and for the first time in my entire life I was penniless. I was totally broke.

Thursday, the day after my experience with the Holy Spirit during the mid-week service, my telephone rang. When I answered, a lady on the other end informed me that she was Pastor Sam Hinn's secretary and that Sam would love to have an opportunity for me to visit with him in his office to share together about our ministries. I was totally in shock. This precious man had never met me and as far as I knew he had never even seen me before, and now he was wanting me to visit with him in his office. Sam's secretary and I set a time for our meeting. It would take place the following Thursday morning at 10:00 A.M.

I will never know how we made it through the next seven days without a cent to our name. My car was nearly out of gas and the groceries were getting dangerously low. My boys still had not given up that expensive habit of eating, much to my disappointment!

It was during that next week that I had finally hit rock bottom. We were now into the third year of our journey through the wilderness. I still remember it as if it were only yesterday, the day that God and I went to battle, and I don't need to tell you who won!

I had become so depressed because of our situation, no money, no sign of anything turning around. I still was not providing for my family as I felt I should. My pride, my self respect, my dignity, it was all gone. It seemed that I had nothing left, and death would have been a welcomed friend.

It was five days before my scheduled appointment with Sam. I was extremely depressed, I was weeping and sobbing, I was laying on the bedroom floor screaming at God. I began to shake my Bible into the face of God—the same

Bible I preach from today. I screamed at him, "You want me to preach this garbage? You want me to tell the people to build their lives on this junk? It is lies; it's all lies. I will never use this book again. I will never preach it to anyone. Where are you in all of this? Why have You been so silent during our desperate time of need? Why have You forsaken me? I can't depend on You. I can't trust You with my life."

Now I know what Jacob must have gone through as he wrestled with the angel of God all night long. It seemed like hours had passed since my encounter with God had begun. I was completely drained. I had nothing left. I was a broken man. And I have learned through that experience it is this very place in our spiritual journey that God desires us all to come. After the severe breaking is complete, then He can put all the tiny pieces back together again and form us into what *He* wants us to be. Thank God for His love, His compassion, His forgiveness, His faithfulness, and His desire to do for us what we are incapable of doing for ourselves.

How very thankful I am today that our God is a God who sees deeply into our hearts and sees what is truly there lying just beneath the surface of all that *stuff*. I can't tell you how many times I have repented over my terrible behavior that day, the horrible way I spoke to such a loving God. He knew it was not me speaking, but it was my desperation speaking. I know He has forgiven me because He tells us in His Word, *"If we confess our sins He is faithful and just to forgive us of our sins and to cleanse us from all unrighteousness"* (1 John 1:9).

I was also reminded that day of 2 Corinthians 4:7-9: *"But we have this treasure in jars of clay to show that this all surpassing power is from God and not from us. We are hard pressed on every side, but not crushed; perplexed, but not in despair; persecuted, but not abandoned; struck down, but not destroyed."*

The apostle Paul continued in verses 16-18: *"Therefore, we do not lose heart. Though outwardly we are wasting away, yet inwardly we are being renewed day by day. For our light and momentary troubles are achieving for us an eternal glory: that far outweighs them all. So we fix our eyes not on what is seen, but on what is unseen. For what is seen is temporary, but what is unseen is eternal."*

It was then that I came to peace with my present situation. God's Word brought me the comfort that I so desperately needed and longed for.

The next day my mother phoned me from her home in Brooksville, Florida. She and my father were the only two people on the planet that knew of our struggles. We shared our situation with no one except for them. She asked, "Barry how are you doing? I answered, "Mom, not so good. Linda and I are penniless for the first time in our married lives, and it is quite frightening."

Mom said that she would put a check in the mail to us that very day. I then said something that even surprised me, I said, "Mom, please don't do it. If you do I will only tear it up. It's not that I wouldn't appreciate it and be extremely grateful; I really would, but it seems that God is trying to teach Linda and me a very important lesson, and we don't want to miss it."

The important lesson that God was attempting to teach us is that He is our provider. He alone is our resource and He can be trusted to provide for our every need no matter what things may look like in the natural.

My mother would later tell us that the hardest thing she ever had to do was to see one of her children in great need and not be able to help them. How thankful Linda and I both are for the loving heart of a godly mother.

It seemed as if the next five days would never end. I was so excited about having an appointment with Brother Sam I could hardly stand it. Finally, Thursday arrived. After my arrival at the church I found my way to Pastor Sam's secretary's desk. I introduced myself, and she said, "Yes, Barry, Brother Hinn is expecting you." She called him on the intercom, and a moment later he stepped from his office. He approached me, gave me a bear hug as if he had known me for years, he shook my hand and said, "I'm Sam Hinn. It is so good to meet Sharon's former pastor." With that we stepped into his office. He took his place behind the desk, and I sat in one of the two side chairs on the opposite side of his desk.

We began our time together with simple small talk just to break the ice. Of course nothing was mentioned about the wilderness journey God had my family and me on. We really had come to understand what Moses had gone through during his forty years on the back side of the desert in his preparation for the task that God had before him. God would later use this eighty-year-old shepherd to deliver His chosen people from their bondage in Egypt, and God would one day use Linda and me to deliver His children from the land of the North and to assist them in their "final return" to the land of Israel—the land of their inheritance. God was using this three-and-one-half years of our wilderness experience as a very important time of preparation.

Perhaps five minutes had passed since entering Sam's office when suddenly out of nowhere I saw Sam's countenance completely change. He had a very strange expression on his face. It was then that he said, "Excuse me Barry, there is something I must do." With that he got up from his desk, walked behind me, and went out to his secretary's desk. I had absolutely no idea what was taking place. I thought that perhaps he had forgotten to do something very important or perhaps he had to make an extremely important phone call. It seemed rather strange that he would interrupt our time together and walk out of his office leaving me alone.

Just a few minutes later he re-entered the office only to lay a green check on the corner of the desk in front of me. He then returned to his chair behind the desk. As I glanced down at the check I noticed it was made payable to me. I didn't look at the amount at that point. I was so surprised that this was the reason he had left the office—it was to have his secretary write a check. I remember saying, "Sam, I can't take this check. This is not why I am here today. In fact, I don't know why I'm here; it was you who made this appointment without even knowing me."

Sam only responded by saying, "Barry, don't argue with me about this. As you were speaking earlier the Holy Spirit told me to write you a check, and He even told me the amount. So if you want to argue with someone over this you will just have to argue with the Holy Spirit. I don't even know if you need this. You may have thousands of dollars lying in the bank, and that's alright if you do. All I know is that I have to be totally obedient to the leading of the Holy Spirit, and He told me to do this for you." I thought to myself, "Oh, Sam, if you only knew."

Keep in mind that absolutely nothing was mentioned about our desperate situation. Only my mother and father knew of what we were going through. I finally glanced down at the check again, and when I saw the amount that it was written out for I almost came unglued. The check was made out for five hundred dollars! Do you remember how much I gave in the offering in that same church eight days earlier? I gave the last five dollars I had in the world. I gave what I had, just as the Holy Spirit had insisted I do. And now, just eight days later God was returning to me one hundredfold what I had given to Him. But why should I be surprised? Why should you be surprised? After all, didn't God tell us in His Word that this is exactly what He would do, if we would only be obedient and trust Him with all we have?

God made us all a promise when Jesus said in Matthew 19:29: *"And everyone who has left houses or brothers or sisters or father or mother or children or fields for my sake will receive (a hundred times) as much and will inherit eternal life."*

There it is. God said I will restore to you a hundredfold what you give to me. Orlando Christian Center did not need

~~the five dollar offering I left there that Wednesday night, but~~ I desperately needed to give it. It was a time of testing and a time of learning that I will never forget.

Praise God for his promises and His faithfulness to those who diligently seek Him and His perfect will for their lives. God will never permit us to come to a place in our lives where He is indebted to us. We will always be indebted to Him for "... *every good and perfect gift is from above*" (James 1:16a).

Chapter Six

The God of Many Miracles

*"Believe me when I say that I am in the Father and
the Father is in me; or at least believe on the
evidence of the miracles themselves."*
John 14:11

It was August of 1992; not much had changed by this time
concerning our financial situation and my "job" hunting.
By now I had taken another temporary job through the
temp employment agency. This time it was with Sun Trust
Bank in Orlando. I was hired to work in their records vault
filing the thousands of loan applications and the paper work
produced from their transactions. It was not an exciting job
to say the least, but it did pay seven dollars per hour, and
it helped me to feel that I was at least doing something in
support of my family.

Shortly after beginning this job, Hurricane Andrew swept
across south Florida leaving a thirty-five mile wide path of
destruction from coast to coast. Thousands of Floridians
lost everything; homes, vehicles, furniture, clothing, jobs,
pets, and in some cases even family members. During my
tour of duty in Viet Nam I had seen many things, and I had
seen much destruction, but I had never—even there—seen
the kind of destruction that Andrew left behind.

I was at the bank one day filing the paper work as usual when suddenly I heard that still small voice of God in my sprit say to me, "Barry, I want you to go to south Florida and help those devastated people put their lives back together, both physically and spiritually."

Having received my orders from "Headquarters" once again, that very week I filed papers to register a non-profit organization with the State of Florida. God even gave me the name of the organization. It would be called "Christian Relief Ministries." So here I was, I had the call to go, I had the organization through which to do the work, BUT still I had no financial resources. I was also in need of a place to stay once I arrived in Cutler Ridge, a community not far from Miami. There were no hotels or motels operational, no electricity, no running water, no restaurants open, no food stores available. The complete infrastructure was gone.

I knew that I didn't want to go to the scene of all that devastation and become a burden on the very people that I was going down there to help. So once again, I did the only thing I knew to do—*I PRAYED*! It was a Friday night. After going to bed that night I had a "business meeting" with God. I prayed, "God I know that you have called me to South Florida to assist in the hurricane relief effort, but I have no place to stay once I arrive there. I need you to provide me with a travel trailer or a motor home to live in while I am there."

The next day was Saturday, which gave me a day off from the bank, and Linda's doctor's office was closed. We had decided to rest for awhile outside in the warm Florida sunshine. About two o'clock in the afternoon my eldest son Barry came to us and said, "Dad there is a phone call for you."

"Do you know who it is?" I asked. "Please take their phone number, and I will return the call when I come in," I instructed him.

Barry became persistent in his pleas for me to go into the house and take the call. He said, "Dad, the caller's name is Peg Babb, and she is insisting on talking to you."

I recognized that name as one of my father's cousins whom I had known all my life, but I had not seen or heard from her in many years. For a number of years as a child both of our families lived on the same street in Burnham, Pennsylvania, which allowed her children, my siblings and me to become good friends. And now after many years of no contact, she was on the phone wishing to speak to me.

I made my way into the house as quickly as possible to take the call. "Peg, it is so good to hear from you after so long. How are you doing?" I asked. She said, "Barry, I am here in Orlando with Sis," (that is her oldest daughter's nickname, who I had not seen as well for many years) "and we were wondering if we could stop by to visit with you and Linda." How nice it was going to be to see both of these dear ladies again and get all caught up on our lives after so many years apart.

Within thirty minutes we heard a knock at the front door. As I opened the door, there stood Peg and her daughter Sis (Carol). It wasn't too long into our conversation that we learned that both of them were Christians and they had been walking close to the Lord for all these years.

At one point Peg said, "Barry, I don't know why, but for about the past two weeks God has really put you and your family on my heart. I have no idea why, but all I knew to do was to lift you in prayer daily. I knew in my spirit that I had to make contact with you after all these years. I phoned your mother, and she gave me your phone number, and since I had to come to Orlando I just took a chance on giving you a call. Now here we are. I know God has ordained our time together today for a Divine purpose."

We continued to enjoy our time together, then Peg asked me where I was pastoring. I admitted that at the present time I did not have a church, but that God had called me to go to south Florida to assist families in the aftermath of Hurricane Andrew. With that I asked her and Carol if they both would join Linda and me in prayer over the next several days asking God to supply me with a travel trailer or a used motor home so I would at least have a roof over my head when I headed to Cutter Ridge to begin my work.

Just as the words "used motor home" left my lips, Carol began to cry. I asked her what the problem was, and she answered by saying, "Now I know why we are here today. Sitting in my driveway over in Titusville is a used 27-foot motor home that my husband Bud and I have been trying to sell for over two years. Now I know why we haven't been able to sell it. God has had it waiting for you. We want you to come by our home and pick it up and use it for as long as you need it." Carol told me she would speak to Bud to see what would be a good time for me to come to their home to take delivery of the motor home.

The next morning I placed a phone call to my third cousin's home and Bud answered the call. When I asked about a time to pick up the motor home, I was so surprised to hear his response. He said, "Barry, Carol and I have given this a great deal of thought since last night, and we have decided that we don't want to loan the motor home to you." Those words sent a chill through my body as I thought my miracle had just been stolen from me by Satan himself.

I told Bud how thankful I was for them to have even considered such a wonderful thing and that I understood perfectly about his decision. He said, "No, I don't think you do understand. We don't want to just *loan* the motor home to you, we want to sign the title over to you and *give* it to you for your ministry."

How could I ever thank God enough for His faithfulness? Just two nights earlier, I went to bed praying for a travel trailer or a motor home, and after my trip to Titusville I had one sitting in my driveway. Praise God, who provides all we have need of to accomplish His perfect will. You see, once again, God was teaching us that He is our provider and we would be able to trust Him no matter what He might call us to do now and in the future.

Here is another very important truth and Kingdom principle we can all glean from this motor home miracle story. God will *never* call any of us to do anything that He does not provide the means to carry out that calling. If God didn't provide ALL we have need of when He calls us to a particular task it would be no different than a father asking his teenage son to go out and mow the lawn and then not give him a mower with which to cut the grass.

I am totally convinced that there are many things in the church of Jesus Christ that are never accomplished because far too many followers of Christ are not willing to step out in child-like faith. They know that God has called them to do a particular thing, but they want everything laid out before them. They want the finances, the workers, the materials, etc. in place before they are willing to do the thing that God has called them to do. And when these things are not right out there in front of them, they refuse to move in response to the orders they received from "Headquarters."

If we need to have everything in hand or laid out before us then there is no need for faith. We would only be able to do the things that we are capable of doing in our own strength and with our own resources. I will never forget what the late Doctor Jerry Falwell once said as he addressed a group of us pastors in Lynchburg, Virginia. He said, *"If you want the world to know that God did it, do something that is far bigger than yourself."* What wonderful counsel from this man of God. This is godly counsel that we can all adopt for our lives and for our ministries. We can—and we should—do mightier and greater things than we have ever done in the past. The writer of the book of Hebrews tells us in Hebrews 11:6a: *"And without faith it is impossible to please God."*

I have always looked to the eleventh chapter of Hebrews to embolden my faith anytime I felt my faith waning. This powerful chapter is known as the "Great Faith Chapter," the Faith Hall of Fame, if you will. Time and space do not allow me to share the many other wonderful miracles that Linda, my sons and I experienced over that three-and-one-half years of wondering on the back side of the desert with God. I can say this with no uncertainty: we are so thankful that we learned the lessons God was teaching us in only three-and-a-half years instead of having to stay in that wilderness for *forty* years. The wilderness was such a powerful place of learning, a place of training, a place of miracles, a place where God had my family and me in a time of preparation for what was to come over the next few years.

I know now that if God had not prepared us in the way He had, we would not have been able to step out on faith as we did when He called us into the former Soviet Union countries to be involved in the re-gathering of His Chosen People from the "Land of the North."

If He had not broken us completely—if He had not brought us to that point of understanding that He could be trusted with our future, that He would provide us with everything we had need of to complete the task that He would eventually call us to do—we would still be pastoring Trinity Assembly of God Church.

During my time in Cutler Ridge ministering to the hurricane victims, helping to rebuild their physical homes and, more importantly, helping them to rebuild their spiritual lives, I would leave my home and family every Monday in the early morning hours to drive five hours to the Miami area to begin my week. Throughout the week I would live in the motor home that God so miraculously provided for me. When 5:00 P.M. Friday evening arrived, I drove the five hours back to Orlando to spend the weekend with my wife and boys. I did this for over eight months, and during that time I was so blessed to have had the opportunity to pray many souls into the wonderful Kingdom of God.

After all, these people had lost everything, and they had no where to turn except to God. They were so open to the Good News of the Gospel for spiritual healing, emotional healing, physical healing, and anything that God had available for them.

Once again, in the valley of despair I witnessed so many miracles that I would not have seen if I had not listened to the voice of God and had not gone by faith to help in the recovery effort of Hurricane Andrew.

You may have been wondering where our finances came from during this eight months in Cutler Ridge. Once again, it was God! It was such a miracle how God brought me together with a Christian contractor named Phil Bland. I had never met Phil until one Sunday evening when Linda and I had decided that we would attend the evening service at Faith Assembly of God in the Orlando area. It was that same evening that I met Phil for the first time, and when I told him what God had called me to do he seemed so surprised. You see, Phil had been called to take his construction skills to the Miami area to help in the recovery effort. That very evening he was assembling a crew of construction workers to go with him to rebuild homes from the foundation up.

Phil was able to offer good wages for his workers, so when he asked me to be a part of this team, I said that I would. Isn't God good? Until I was willing to step out on faith I had no idea where my finances would come from, but God did. The very next day I was on my way to Cutler Ridge answering the call of God on my life with everything I had need of already provided by the God of miracles.

Chapter Seven

The Time of Preparation Continues

A New Place, a New Assignment

After being in Cutler Ridge for eight months, driving back and forth to be with my family on the weekends, God was moving behind the scenes to redirect me once again.

One day when I was still on the job rebuilding homes and lives, my cell phone rang. It was a call from my Presbyter, Rev. Carl Stephens, who is also the Pastor of Faith Assembly of God, the same church where I had met Phil Bland just eight months earlier. Pastor Stephens is also Phil's brother-in-law. I had known Pastor Stephens for about three years, ever since I had my ministerial credentials transferred into the Assemblies of God from the Church of the Nazarene.

His purpose for phoning me that day was to ask me if I would be willing to meet the church board of Trinity Assembly of God Church. The church was situated in a small community a few miles east of Orlando.

After telling him I would be happy to meet with the board, he made the necessary arrangements for the meeting to take place. The evening of the meeting with the board

Linda and I drove onto the church property for the first time. When we parked the car in the parking lot something miraculous happened to both of us at the very same time. It was a witness of the Holy Spirit. Without having met anyone associated with that church, without having seen the inside of the church or the parsonage which sat on the same five-acre plot of land, we both knew in the depths of our beings that this was where God would have us labor.

After a very warm and blessed meeting with the church board members, they extended an invitation to me to preach for them the following Sunday morning and evening. We accepted the offer with much gladness because we already knew without any doubt whatsoever that this was the place for our next assignment.

Our first service with this group of wonderful people was such a blessing. The service went well, and we could hardly wait until we could go back that evening. At the close of the service we all had a wonderful time around the altar seeking God's direction for the church and for the Wagner family. As the assistant presbyter had the church body cast their votes for us, there was no doubt in our minds as to what the outcome of the vote would be. Please understand that it wasn't because we thought so much of ourselves that we already knew the outcome of the vote. No, God had already broken us of self pride and everything else of which we needed to be broken. We knew what the outcome of the vote would be because God had already confirmed it in our hearts that first night when we pulled onto the property to meet with the board.

After the assistant presbyter had counted the votes he announced to the congregation and to the board that we had received a unanimous vote. We had just been called to be the new spiritual leaders of the Trinity Assembly of God Church where we would serve gladly for the next five-and-one-half years, *until God* would once again say *go*.

Throughout our ministry God has always used Linda and me to go into a struggling church situation, breathe new life into the work, remodel the church building and usually the parsonage as well, and Trinity was no exception. At one point in our years of ministry God called us from a successful pastorate to pioneer a brand new work. What a challenge it was, but we did it gladly.

When we arrived at Trinity we found that there was no money in the bank, and there was a mortgage on the church, the property, and the parsonage. The church also had a loan to the district which was past due, and they were not even able to make minimum payments on it. The former pastor had not received a salary in over eight months. The church had just received an insurance settlement for hail damage on the church roof, but instead of putting a new roof on the church, they paid all the back wages to the outgoing pastor, which of course was the right thing to do, *but* it left us with a very difficult situation and a terrific challenge.

At the time of our taking over the leadership roll of the church it had been supporting only six missionaries on a monthly basis. I knew immediately this would have to change. From the earliest days of my conversion experience God had given me a real heart for missions.

So it was with so many other churches that we had pastored in the past, we all rolled up our sleeves, and we hit the ground running. The church structure and the parsonage were in serious need of repairs. With approval of the church board we went to our local bank; we secured a loan and began to put a new face on Trinity Assembly of God.

After many months of hard work, sweat, and even a few tears along the way, the church, the out building, and the parsonage were completely renovated. Thank God for the many wonderful lay people who gave of their time, their finances and their God-given talents to assist in this much-needed metamorphosis. Without them we could never have accomplished what was essential if the church was ever to grow in numbers, finances, support of additional missionaries and local ministries.

By the time God finished using us at Trinity Assembly of God, He had blessed our church with capacity-filled services, many new souls born into the Kingdom, a great number of baptisms, a great increase in finances, a wonderful spirit in the church, and a congregation that truly felt like family to one another. Our monthly missionary support grew from supporting six missionaries per month to supporting forty-two. God is so good, and He can accomplish so much when His people are willing to put their hands to the plow and simply do what they are called to do. God will *always* add the increase.

Chapter Eight

My Heart Was Strangely Warmed

*"Whoever obeys His command will come to no harm,
and the wise HEART will know the
proper time and procedure."*
Ecclesiastes 8:5

One Saturday evening in April of 1998, the front doorbell rang at the parsonage. As I approached the glass paneled door I was able to see a couple standing on the front porch and recognized them as Steve and Reba, who were dear friends we had met in Israel a few years earlier on one of our many trips.

As the evening unfolded, we eventually gathered around the diningroom table for refreshments, coffee, and a time of fellowship and sharing. Reba told us that she had just returned home from a very emotional trip to Ukraine where she was able to travel with a photo journalist aboard a ship taking hundreds of Jewish immigrants to Israel.

As she shared the many pictures that she had taken of the Jewish people aboard the ship during this godly adventure, I became aware that something was happening in my spirit. With each picture I looked at, this thing that I was feeling became more and more intense. At one point I even began to cry as I looked into the faces of these precious people who where on their way home from the "Land of the North" in fulfillment of many Bible prophecies.

I wanted Reba to tell me every little detail of her trip. "Don't leave anything out," I said. "Tell me everything." The more she spoke the more God was drawing me into the events that she had been able to capture so wonderfully well on film, and I felt that my heart had been strangely warmed.

Having walked with the Lord for many years by this point I was mature enough in the faith to realize that what I was experiencing was a move of God in my life.

At that particular moment I wasn't quite certain of what all this meant or what it would eventually lead to in the not-so-distant future. Before Steve and Reba left our home that night I made certain that I was given all of the contact information concerning the organization that was operating this ship of freedom for the Jewish people. I was informed that the ship was being operated by Ebenezer Emergency Fund, a non-denominational Christian organization based in England. The ship they had contracted was sailing two times a month from the Port of Odessa, Ukraine, to the Port of Haifa, Israel.

When I woke up the next morning the events of the previous night were still very heavy on my heart. Something, or Someone (could it have been the Holy Spirit?) was making it very clear to me that I had to make contact with this organization.

Making my initial call to England, I was told they would send me a volunteer's packet in the mail. I was to pray about becoming a volunteer with them, fill out the forms if I felt this was God's leading, return the forms, and wait for an answer. If I was accepted it would be for a period of three months during the summer—June, July and August.

Upon receipt of the registration forms I quickly filled them out, gathered the required personal recommendation letters from a fellow pastor and friends, and quickly put them back into the mail. Now, all I could do was to wait and pray.

A few days later while in prayer about the possibility of serving as a volunteer with Ebenezer Emergency Fund, a good dose of reality hit me squarely between the eyes. I realized that if I was accepted for this work I would have to go to my church board and ask them to release me for twelve weeks. Oops, could this be a hurdle that would keep me from doing what I truly felt so certain that God was calling me to do? So now, I had something else to pray about over the next few weeks.

The next two or three weeks seemed like an eternity to me as I not so patiently waited for the answer to my application to arrive. *FINALLY* it came. With shaking hands I opened the large white envelope and began to read the cover letter with a great deal of anxiety. "Dear Rev. Wagner, we are most happy to inform you that you have been accepted to serve as a volunteer in Odessa, Ukraine, for a period of three months. You will be on a team of other volunteers from all over the world for the months of June, July and August." Praise the Lord!! I had cleared the first hurdle.

Now, it was time for hurdle number two. If I thought the first hurdle was set at a high level, surely hurdle number two would be even higher. After all, I was the senior pastor. What church board would ever release their senior pastor to go halfway around the world to be involved in another ministry for three solid months? Had I missed the leading of God? Did I clearly hear the voice of the Holy Spirit? Time would soon give me an answer to these most important questions.

The church's monthly board meeting was scheduled for the following week. It would be at this meeting that I would have an opportunity to share my heart with my board members. As the day of the meeting approached I spent a great deal of time in prayer knowing that if it was God's will for me to labor among His people in Ukraine, He would have to clear the way for me.

The packet of materials I received in the mail included a thirty minute video about the work of Ebenezer. I watched that video over and over again during the days leading up to the board meeting. It had totally captured my heart. It was as if I were viewing it through Father's eyes. Oh, how it ministered to me concerning the *aliyah*, the return of the Jews to Israel.

The evening of the board meeting finally arrived. I felt that God was directing me to show that same video to my board members, but it had to be covered with prayer. I remember asking God to help my board to view the video in the same way that He had allowed me to view it—through His eyes.

As the meeting began, I hurried through the other business at hand so I could get to the thing that was dear to my heart. I spent about thirty minutes simply sharing what God had been doing in my spirit about the return of the Jewish people to their homeland.

Then I showed the board the thirty-minute video, but before I did, I prayed with them, "Dear God, please allow these godly men to view this video through your eyes. Amen." I must tell you, while the film was playing, I spent that entire thirty minutes in serious prayer for I understood that this group of men could prevent me from responding to God's call on my life if they voted the wrong way.

When the film had finished I asked the men to share with me whatever was on their hearts concerning the need to release me for three months. One by one in turn, they went around the table sharing their sincere feelings. Much to my surprise, every one of the men's comments was extremely positive. I was totally amazed when the last board member said, "Pastor Wagner, we have sensed your heart and your spirit about this. If we do not release you to do what you know God is calling you to do, we will not be fighting against

Pastor Wagner. We would be fighting against God, and we don't wish to be in that position. Go with our blessings."

My friends, when God places a call on your life, you can be certain that He will make a way where there seems to be no way. My board not only gave me a three months sabbatical leave of absence, but they blessed me even more by telling me that they would continue paying me my weekly salary in full during those three months while away. God is so faithful!

The next few weeks passed quickly as I made all the necessary preparations for my departure for Odessa, Ukraine. Of course the most difficult thing I would have to deal with was saying good-bye to Linda and the boys. It would be three months before I could be with them again.

I am so thankful to God that He has blessed me with the most supportive wife a man could ever hope to have. Linda knew that God had placed this call on my life, and she wasn't about to allow her personal feelings get in the way of what God was doing. When it comes to ministry, we both learned many years earlier that whatever God calls us to do, the *"cost is never greater than the cause."* We have tried our very best during our thirty-three years of full-time ministry to labor in Kingdom work with that conviction, and it has served us well.

The time for my departure had finally arrived. I was now on my way to fulfill God's calling for my life as I would labor among His chosen people in Odessa, Ukraine.

I would be less than honest if I didn't tell you that it was not easy saying good-bye to Linda and my boys, realizing that I would not see them again for three months. The thing that made it possible for us to part was that we all knew this was a holy work and a holy calling that God had directed me to do. Once again, I had received my orders from "Headquarters." I had—no *we* had—no other choice but to step out in faith and obedience to do the will of God.

Anytime God speaks and gives us marching orders we have one of two choices to make. One, we can refuse those orders and basically say, "God, I hear your voice, but I really don't want to do that, or I really don't want to go there, or I'm not willing to pay the price that would be required of me to carry out those orders." Or we can say, "Yes, Lord, here am I."

Does all of this sound familiar to you? It should. We have all heard someone else respond to God's call in the same way as it is recorded in the book of Exodus. That's right; it was Moses, God's appointed man, whom God was calling to a task that would change the life of an entire nation forever. And what did God hear from Moses when he was called? Excuses—one excuse after another as to why he was *not* the person who should be carrying out such orders.

Moses received his marching orders from "Headquarters" in Exodus 3:10: *"So now, go. I am sending you to Pharaoh to bring my people, the Israelites out of Egypt."*

And what was this great, future leader's response to God's call on his life? In Exodus 3:11 we hear Moses say to God, *"Who am I, that I should go to Pharaoh and bring the Israelites out of Egypt?"*

In verse thirteen, once again, Moses says to God, *"Suppose I go to the Israelites and say to them, 'The God of your fathers has sent me to you,' and they ask me, 'What is his name?' Then what shall I tell them?"*

Moses again responds to God in Exodus 4:1: *"What if they do not believe me or listen to me and say, 'The Lord did not appear to you'?"*

Still not being able to convince God that he was not the right man for the job, Moses tries a fourth time by saying in Exodus 4:10: *"O Lord, I have never been eloquent, neither in the past nor since you have spoken to your servant. I am slow of speech and tongue."*

Finally, after four feeble attempts to persuade God that He really had far better people other than himself to call for this important mission, the real *truth* finally comes out. In Exodus 4:13 Moses finally becomes totally honest with God when he says, *"O Lord, please send someone else to do it."*

There it is! The truth of the matter was that Moses just *didn't want to do it!* He had thrown out every possible excuse as to why God should not call him for such a task. Moses was looking for God to let him off the hook because he was having trouble realizing that he was God's man for that critical hour. Moses was convinced that God was about to make His very first mistake by placing this call upon him.

How many of us have been convinced of the same thing as Moses. "Surely God, you are not calling me to do such a thing!" And then the excuses begin to fly.

I really believe there are a few lessons for us all to learn from this story of Moses. The first lesson is this, *God does not make mistakes!* If He calls *you* to do a particular task it *is you* that He wants for that assignment, not the person *you* think would be better for the job. God knows how unique you really are. After all it was He who created you. He created you with special talents and spiritual gifts, and He knows how they can be best used in the Kingdom-building business.

A second lesson we can learn from this account of Moses' call is that *"when God calls, He supplies."* As mentioned in an earlier chapter, God will never call us to a task that He does not provide the resources to carry it out; however, the provisions required will not begin to flow into your life until you are willing to step out in child-like faith.

A third lesson to be gleaned from this story is that it displeases the heart of God when we say *no* to Him. Did you notice how God responded to the objections of Moses? In Exodus 4:14 we read: *"Then the Lord's anger burned against Moses."* At this point, God was not very happy with His servant Moses. Not a good place to be.

Now on the other hand, the second choice we have when we hear the voice of God calling us to a particular task is this: we can respond in perfect obedience to God's call as Isaiah did in Isaiah 6:8: *Then, I heard the voice of the Lord saying, "Whom shall I send? And who will go for us?" And I said, "Here am I, Send me!"* This is the response that greatly pleases the heart of Abba.

So, the long and the short of it is simple. When God places a call on our lives, we really have only two choices. We can respond by saying either *yes* or *no*. We can respond by being obedient or disobedient. We can respond as Moses did with one excuse after another, *or* we can respond as Isaiah did by simply saying, *"Here am I; send me!"* The choice is ours. Let's pray that we will always respond in the way that pleases and blesses the heart of God! It should always be our desire to walk and move and have our being in the *perfect will* of God.

Part 2

The First Taste of Aliyah

Chapter Nine

The Work of Aliyah Begins

*"See, I will bring them from the land of the north
and gather them from the ends of the earth.
Among them will be the blind and the lame,
expectant mothers and women in labor;
a great throng will return."*
Jeremiah 31:8

Upon my arrival at the Odessa airport in Ukraine, I was greeted by two volunteers whose three-month stay was about to end. On the thirty-minute ride to Yunost, the base where I would be assigned, these two "veterans" filled me in on what I could expect during my stay. By the time we arrived at the base I felt like I just wanted to hit the ground running by getting started on what God had sent me there to do—to assist in the *aliyah* and to be a special blessing to the Jewish people.

There was such a sense of anticipation coursing through my innermost being. I knew that I was exactly where God wanted me to be at this time in my life and my ministry. I strongly believe that this is one of the most important things for every believer to know—that they are walking in the *perfect will* of God.

As I have traveled around the world speaking in churches and doing conferences over these past nine years, I have met so many wonderful Christians of all ages who feel that God is placing a call on their life but they don't know what that call is. They will share with me how frustrated they are because they are so willing to do whatever God is calling them to do. They are willing to go anywhere in the world to do whatever God wants them to do. I think that one of the hardest things for any fully committed Christian to do is to *wait* on the Lord.

You have given your life completely over to God. The most important thing for you now is to know His perfect will for your life and then to walk in it. But you pray and you pray, asking over and over again, "Dear God, what are you calling me to do? I am ready to go and to do whatever it is you may have for me." Perhaps you have been there in the past or perhaps you may find yourself in that position as you are reading these words. If this is where you are presently in your walk with God, I want to encourage you to *not* give up. Keep praying and realize a couple of important Kingdom truths. First, God's delays are not God's denials. And secondly, God's timing is perfect. He is never early, but He is *never* late either.

As you pray seeking God's leading for your life, ask Him to give you clarity concerning the call He is placing on your life. Ask Him to make it so clear to you that there is no possibility of missing it. Another very important thing to ask when you pray is for God to show you His heart. Ask Him what is the nearest and the dearest thing to His heart.

So many times we think we know what God would have us do. We put all of *our* plans together, we lay out a time table, and then we lay it all before the Lord and say, "Dear God, please bless this." In reality this may not be what God wants to bless at all. While it may be a good project or a good ministry, we may be missing God completely.

Over my many years of ministry I have learned that I really don't want God to bless what *"I"* want to do or what *"I"* think He wants me to do. I want to *know* what His *perfect will* is. I want to know *His* heart, and once that is revealed then I can ask Him to bless my work as I step into it.

So continue praying without ceasing, continue asking and continue seeking His heart. Then in His time, at His appointed time, I can assure you the answer will come with such clarity you will know with no uncertainty that you have heard from the very heart of Abba.

I realize that we just took a small side track from the story of my arrival in Odessa, but I am certain that there are many fully committed believers reading this book right now who have been struggling with this most important issue. If even one of you has been helped by what was said above, then the time was well spent. I guess that is the pastor coming out of me. Now, let's get back to Odessa.

The next three months proved to be some of the most exciting and blessed months of my entire life. Many times the work was physically challenging and difficult but, oh, so rewarding. It is impossible to pour your heart and your life out for others without being extremely blessed in the process, and this is doubly true when you are being a blessing to the Jewish people, the Apple of His eye. *"... For whoever touches you [Israel] touches the apple of His eye"* (Zechariah 2:8b NIV). And Jesus said it this way, *"Verily I say unto you, inasmuch as ye have done it unto one of the least of these my brethren, [a Jewish person], ye have done it unto me"* (Matthew 25:40 KJV).

The volunteer team that God assembled in Odessa came from many different countries of the world. They came from England, America, Germany, Australia, New Zealand and South Africa. While we all came from different countries and different cultures the common denominator that made us one was that we all shared the heart of the Father for the Jewish people and the land of Israel. We all had come to be servants and to be a blessing to the Jewish people of the former Soviet Union. Matthew 20:26-28 tells us: *"Not so with you. Instead, whoever wants to become great among you must be your servant, and whoever wants to be first must be your slave—just as the Son of Man did not come to be served, but to serve, and to give his life as a ransom for many."*

It was early into my three-month "tour of duty" when I found myself with the team at the central railroad station in Odessa at 4:30 A.M. We had arrived early that morning to meet the Jewish people we were assisting in their departure to Israel who were arriving by train from various parts of the former Soviet Union (FSU). It was then that I met a precious elderly Jewish woman who I fell in love with immediately. She was making *aliyah* with her daughter and her granddaughter. Her name was Sofia, and she was seventy-nine years old.

When I first spotted her she was standing at the top of the steps of the train preparing to make her descent to the station platform. I couldn't help but notice that she was carrying a white walking cane with a red tip on the end, and I realized that this lovely little lady was totally blind. It was then that the Holy Spirit reminded me of Jeremiah 31:8: *"See, I will bring them from the land of the north* [Russia] *and gather them from the ends of the earth. Among them will be the* blind *and the lame, expectant mothers and women in labor; a great throng will return"* (emphasis mine).

I ran up the four steps of the train to put myself on the same level as Sofia. I said in the Russian language, "Good morning, my name is Barry Wagner, and I am here to help you." I took her by the arm and helped her down the steps to the platform. After introducing myself to her daughter and granddaughter and after recovering their luggage, we were off to the waiting transport vans that would take us to

Yunost where we would care for them until the day when we would set sail for Israel.

The ship was not scheduled to sail for another week, and it was during that time that the God of Abraham, Isaac and Jacob knitted my heart with Sofia's and hers with mine. Anytime I saw Sofia come into the dining room I would get up from my seat at the table and go to her. I would greet her by saying, "Good morning Sofia, it's me, Barry. May I escort you to your seat?" At the sound of my voice and anytime she heard my name, a wonderful smile appeared across her aged face.

I would take her arm in mine, and we would walk across that diningroom together. I felt as if I was escorting a queen to her throne, and I was. As we approached her chair, I would pull it out and help her take her seat. This became our routine for every meal after that. I could tell that little Sofia for the first time in her life felt like she was really something special. And she was! She was very special to me, and she was extremely special to God. *"As you have done it unto the least of these my brethren, you have done it unto me,"* Jesus said.

Anytime I saw this lovely Jewish woman walking the grounds of the camp with her daughter or sitting on one of the park benches, I would always make a point to go to her and say, "Hello Sofia, it's me, Barry." Sofia would light up, and that beautiful smile would once again appear across her face. In turn that smile lit up my heart in such a beautiful way that I cannot fully explain, but I know it's a sight that I will never forget.

One Sunday morning as I came from my second floor dormitory room to the flower garden just outside, I saw Sofia sitting on one of the benches all alone. She was sitting quietly enjoying the warm sun of a beautiful summer morning and listening to the sounds of the birds as they flew from tree to tree.

I made my way over to where she was sitting and once again I said, "Good morning Sofia; it's Barry." And as always her entire face became radiant. I took a place beside her on the bench and I began to speak to her in English. I knew very little Russian in 1998. I knew she didn't understand a word I was saying. She spoke back to me in her native tongue, and of course I didn't understand a word that she was saying, but I want you to know something very important. Sofia and I were communicating that morning.

Please allow me to take a little side step at this point to share a very important lesson that many of us learned while laboring there in Odessa among the Russian-speaking Jews.

The volunteer team that I had been a part of was into about our seventh week of our "Tour of Duty" since our arrival in Odessa. Since I was the only pastor on the team, if one of the other volunteers was experiencing difficulty or if they had a personal problem of some sort, they would come to me. I guess it just goes with the territory, but I was always happy to listen and to help whenever I could.

One afternoon following a full day's work among the immigrants, two of our young ladies came to me to share a very real frustration they were both trying to deal with. Both of these lovely ladies had such a love for the Apple of God's eye, and they wanted to be as effective in their ministry to them as they could possibly be. Both girls were in their early twenties. Heidi was from Australia, and Ingrid was from New Zealand.

They began explaining to me how disappointed they felt that their time up to this point was not as rewarding as they had hoped it would be. I asked, "What do you mean girls? We are so blessed to be here and to be serving the many hundreds of Jewish people that God has honored us to be with." The girls went on to share with me how they wished so badly to be sharing their lives and their hearts with these precious people, but because they did not speak Russian and the immigrants didn't speak English, it was impossible to communicate with them.

"It seems like all we have been able to do these past seven weeks is to carry their luggage for them. We don't mind doing that at all, but we can't verbally communicate with them," the girls explained.

I responded by saying, "Oh no girls, you are so wrong about that. I want you to try something from today forward and just see if it makes a difference in how you feel about what you are doing here. Are you willing to try what I am about to suggest?" Both girls said that they would be willing to try.

The memory of my beautiful experience with Sofia on that Sunday morning was still very fresh in my mind. I said, "Ladies, any time you see some of the *Olim* (immigrants) sitting in the garden or walking around the base, go to them, sit down beside them or begin to walk with them and just start talking as though you have known them for years. Of course you know that they will not be able to understand a word you are saying. They, in turn, will begin speaking back to you in the Russian language, and you won't understand a word of that either, but I can tell you this. You will be *communicating* with them. You see God has His own language and it is spelled L – O – V – E! You will be speaking in the language of God's Holy Spirit, and these wonderful people will sense the love you have for them. Many will be moved to tears because someone cared enough to spend quality time with them and to treat them with dignity."

Not only did Heidi and Ingrid begin to do what was suggested, but the rest of the team did as well. It totally eliminated the frustration that everyone was experiencing, and it changed the atmosphere of the entire base. Now, let's get back to lovely Sofia.

I could tell by Sofia's voice and by her body language that she wanted in some way to repay me for the kindness that I had shown her for nearly a week now. Of course, this precious little Jewish lady had so little in way of worldly possessions to give to anyone, and even if she had I would not have taken a thing from her. After all, it was I who came to give, to show the unconditional love of God to one of His precious people.

And then it happened! Sofia gave me the only thing in this world that she had. She gave me a wonderful gift from herself.

For the next twenty minutes or so she serenaded me in the Russian language. I couldn't understand a word she was singing, but the more she sang to me the more I cried and the more I cried the more she sang. My friends, let me tell you that all the riches of this world cannot compare to what I received early that Sunday morning in 1998 from a poor elderly Ukrainian Jewish woman that touched my heart in such a profound way. What a blessing it was! It is a time and a memory that I will carry with me into eternity.

When the day of sailing arrived there was a great sense of excitement in the air around the base. Our new Jewish friends realized that their long-awaited new life in Israel was about to begin. After just three-and-a-half days at sea the ship would dock in Israel, and they would finally be "home."

The day's activities were very well organized by the base team members, as usual. The transport buses arrived at just the precise time. The luggage (tons of it) as well as the precious human cargo of passengers were boarded onto the waiting buses for their forty-minute drive to the Port of Odessa where their ship to freedom was waiting for their arrival.

It was estimated that on any given sailing day with four hundred to four hundred and fifty *Olim* (Jewish immigrants) leaving for Israel the volunteer team loaded over seventeen tons of luggage by hand. And this day was no exception.

After the many hours required for the loading of luggage, for the immigrants to clear passport control and customs, it was time for them to say goodbye to the only land they had ever known as home. They would soon cease being Ukrainians, or Russians, or Moldovians, etc. and they would all instantly become one. They would all become Israelis the very moment their feet touched Israeli soil for the first time.

It was the following Sunday night when this ship to freedom finally docked at the Port of Haifa, Israel, and the unloading process began. It would take several hours for the volunteer team to unload the many tons of luggage and all of the Jewish immigrants that the God of Abraham, Isaac, and Jacob had called home to their "Promised Land," fulfilling prophetic Scripture. These were people who were participating in the "Final Return" of the Jewish people from all the nations.

These were Jews who had been living in the Diaspora. These were the descendants of the Jewish people who were scattered all over the world when the Holy Temple and the entire city of Jerusalem were destroyed by General Titus of the 10th Roman legion in 70 A.D. And now, just as the prophetic Scriptures said would happen, they were coming *home* to Eretz Israel (the land of Israel) in their "Final Return."

The literal translation of the word *Diaspora* means, "without a covering." If a person is without a covering, without a roof over their head, they are homeless. For two thousand years the Jewish people had been homeless with no homeland to call their own. That was until one of the greatest miracles of all time took place. God re-established the Jewish State of Israel on May 14, 1948. The Bible asks the question, *"Can a country be born in a day or a nation be brought forth in a moment?"* (Isaiah 66:8). I always answer that question this way, "Yes, when God's in it!" How can anyone truly believe that God has turned His back on the Jewish people?

If God has rejected the Jews and broken His covenant with them as the "Replacement Theology" crowd preaches, why is it then that Israel is the only nation in the history of mankind that once was, then wasn't for two thousand years, and now is again? And if God is finished with the Jewish people, why is it that the Hebrew language once was, and then wasn't for nearly two thousand years, and now is again?

The stupendous task of resurrecting the Hebrew language for use in the modern world was undertaken by Eliezer Ben Yehuda. He dedicated his entire life to the task, painstakingly translating every word. His work was scoffed at by modern secular society, who had no desire to learn to speak Hebrew. The religious sector regarded it as sacrilege to bring the language of the sacred writings into public use as a common language of the streets.

The passion for the work he had undertaken was inspired by God. Unknown to Ben Yehuda, he was fulfilling the Word of God for this appointed time in history. When people from one hundred different countries united under the banner of Israel, they could not converse, so a common language was a necessity. It was decided to reinstate the Hebrew language to unite the State of Israel as one people. It is an interesting fact that Hebrew is the only language in the world that does not have any swear words in it. It is a pure language as the Bible states. Prophecy was therefore fulfilled when this language was resurrected!

Chapter Ten

Another Early Morning at the Station

*"Comfort, comfort my people, says your God.
Speak tenderly to Jerusalem, and proclaim to her that
her time of exile has ended."*
Isaiah 40:5

I must tell you that before I began my volunteer work in Odessa, I didn't even realize that there was a 4:00 A.M. But I learned very quickly during my stay there that the days began extremely early. As a pastor of over twenty five years it was customary for my day at the church to begin at 8:00 A.M., so this was something quite foreign to me. But when God has you on assignment you find that the living conditions—the different foods, the early morning hours, the different culture, etc.—aren't really all that important. Remember? "The cost is never greater than the cause."

It had become quite routine by now to find myself at the central railroad station in Odessa waiting for the trains to arrive with their precious human cargo on board—the Jewish people from many different areas of the FSU.

The train I was assigned to wait for finally pulled into the station from Crimea, which is in the southernmost part of Ukraine. I would be taking from that train several Olim who would be leaving Ukraine on the next sailing to Israel. Along with several others I met that morning was a lovely couple in their early sixties who had lived in Crimea all of their lives. The man's name was Alexander, and his wife was Svetlana.

I was quite surprised when Svetlana greeted me in English. When I had complimented her on her exceptionally good English she told me that she had taught high school English for over forty years.

During our brief conversation I learned that Alexander had recently broken three ribs and was unable to do any heavy lifting. This was not really a problem for us because we always made it a special point to carry everyone's heavy bags for them. Once again, we went to Odessa to be servants to the Jewish people, not to be served. After their bags had all been accounted for we headed for the transport vans for our ride to the base.

Upon our arrival at the base we handed out everyone's room assignments, and later it would become clear that God had orchestrated the room that this couple would stay in until sailing day. The room they were assigned to was just down the hall from the room that my roommate and I shared on the second floor of the dormitory.

One afternoon I was sitting in the dayroom just across from my room. I was reading my Bible, praying and singing in English and in the Spirit. I was lost in a deep place of worship with God and not really conscious of what was taking place around me. By this time Svetlana, her husband, and I had come to know each other quite well. Svetlana knew that the entire volunteer team were all Christians, a fact we never hid from them. While it was the policy of the organization I was a volunteer with not to evangelize, proselyte or attempt to convert any one, we did speak often of the God of Abraham, Isaac and Jacob.

That afternoon while I was deep in worship with this God of Abraham, Isaac and Jacob, Svetlana had come from her room and had taken a seat on the other end of the sofa where I was sitting. She was so gracious. She never spoke a word until I had finished my wonderful time with the Lord. And then she said something that I will remember for the rest of my life. She said with a sense of disappointment in her voice, "Barry, I don't know this God of Abraham, Isaac and Jacob that you speak of in a personal way as you seem to know Him." My friends, we will never fully understand how our lives lived out for God affect people around us. This precious lady saw something in my life that was missing in hers. It was that personal relationship with a personal God.

After hearing such a statement from one of my newest friends I said, "Svetlana, wait here for just a moment." With that I got up from the sofa and located a Bible—*the Tanakh*—and gave it to her as a gift. I said, "Svetlana this is God's book. It is a spiritual book. It is His love letter to us. If you will read the words of this Holy Book, God will personally reveal Himself to you through His Word, and you, too, will come to know Him in a personal way.

It was two days later that we set sail with another ship-load of Jewish immigrants from the FSU, and Svetlana and her husband were two of the passengers.

Again, the ship docked in Haifa on a Sunday evening, and the unloading process began. I was standing at the bottom of the steps that ran down the side of the ship that were used for the passengers to disembark. At one point during the course of the evening I looked to the top of the steps and spotted Svetlana and Alexander about to descend. As quickly as I could, I shot to the top of the steps and took Svetlana by the hand. As we began our descent down the steps we both understood that we were just moments from having to say good-bye to each other. There was a heaviness in both of our hearts.

After reaching the dock, the three of us stepped out of the way of others coming off the ship. I hugged Alexander and told him good-bye. I then turned to Svetlana; she put her arms around me, and as we stood there embracing one another she began to cry. I could feel her tears warming my back as they fell onto my shirt. I, too, began to cry, and my tears fell down her back. We both knew that apart from a miracle we would never see each other again. In just a few seconds she and Alexander would make their way into the customs hall where I was not permitted to go, and we would not see one another again.

I will never forget the very last words she spoke to me that night. For a second time she said, "Barry, I really do not know the God of Abraham, Isaac and Jacob in the same personal way that you do, but I know that I will very soon."

Having said that and wiping tears from her eyes, Svetlana and Alexander walked out of my life. I have not seen or even heard from this very special couple since that warm summer night in 1998, but if I know anything about God, I know that Svetlana has come to know the God of Abraham, Isaac and Jacob, Who she was so eager to know in a personal way.

One of the most difficult aspects of what I was doing as a volunteer for those three months in Odessa was saying good-bye to the several thousand Jewish people that I had come to know during my work among them.

As I poured my life and my heart into each one of these wonderful people, we truly became one. It was like saying good-bye to a family member, knowing that I would probably never see them again.

Perhaps you have picked up on a very important fact as it pertains to our work with the wonderful Jewish people of the former Soviet Union countries. And what I am about to say pertains to every organization that is now working in this Holy work or has labored in this work in the past. No one and no organization evangelizes the Jewish people we work with. There are *no* hidden agendas, only the response on our part to fulfill the call of God on our lives and our ministries, to love the Jewish people unconditionally. We stand with them and assist them in practical ways to make their *aliyah* to Israel possible.

There are two very important reasons for this. One is that every organization works hand-in-hand with the Jewish agencies in the countries we are laboring in. We do this with the understanding that we are not working with their people for any other reason than to love them and to be a blessing to them as they make their way home to Israel.

It is extremely vital that we retain this trust relationship with the Jewish agencies in all of the former Soviet Union countries that we are laboring in, and in Latin America as well. It is these Jewish agencies that give us the names and the addresses of the Jewish people who are seeking to return to Israel. Without this assistance from the agencies, it would be impossible for us to help any of God's chosen people. We could not feed them, provide them with necessary medications, cloth them, or provide financial assistance to make their *aliyah* that God Himself has ordained for them. They would remain stranded behind the former Iron Curtain, never to realize their God-appointed destiny for their lives.

The second reason we do not evangelize is because as an organization God has not called us to that area of ministry. God makes it very clear throughout the writings of the prophets that He will reveal Himself to them once they are back in their own land.

There are many Scriptures that speak of this great truth, but please hear what God is saying in Ezekiel 36:24-28. *Please* take notice how many times the word "I" is used. The word "I" throughout these Scriptures is speaking of God. *"For I will take you out of the nations; I will gather you from all the countries and bring you back into your own land. I will sprinkle clean water on you, and you will be clean; I will cleanse you from all your impurities and from all your idols. I will give you a new heart and put a new spirit in you; I will put my Spirit in you and move you to follow my decrees and be careful to keep my laws. You will live in the land I gave your forefathers; you will be my people, and I will be your God.*"

I think Jesus said it best in John 4:37: *"Thus the saying 'One sows and another reaps' is true."* We have been called forth to be the sowers, not the reapers. What are we sowing? We are sowing the unconditional love of Christ, and we are sowing the truths of Torah into their lives. God has made it very clear. He wants His children to return to the land of their inheritance, and without the financial assistance the Christian organizations are giving the Jewish people, they would never be able to return.

In the above Scriptures God tells us that after they are in their homeland, Israel, it will be then that He reveals Himself to them, and He will put His Spirit (the Holy Spirit) in them. He tells us that it will be *He* who does it.

I know this seems to be a new way of looking at things as far as this matter is concerned. I will be the first to agree with you. As a long-time pastor of the Assemblies of God denomination I have always preached, lived, eaten, slept, walked and done evangelism, and I still do as far as it pertains to ministry to the Gentile world.

God really had to do a new work in me and help me to understand what He wanted me to do among the Jewish people of the FSU. He made it very clear to me that I would not be doing ministry as I had become so accustomed to doing for many years. God has shown us through the Scriptures that He has, in fact, called certain people and certain organizations to help get His children home to Israel and to simply be the sowers of Christ's unconditional love into these precious people's lives and into their hearts, and His Holy Spirit would do the rest.

Chapter Eleven

The Power of God's Word Confirmed

*"For the word of God is living and active. Sharper than any double-edged sword, it penetrates even to dividing soul and spirit, joints and marrow; it judges the thoughts and attitudes of the **heart**."*
Hebrews 4:12

The above Scripture is so familiar to us all. It is not necessary for a person to be a believer for very long until they are exposed to this wonderful truth from the Word of God.

It is a Scripture I have read and preached for over thirty years, and yet it wasn't until July of 1998 that I saw this verse miraculously come alive. It was then that I became fully aware of what the writer of Hebrews was speaking about.

I was sailing on the ship out of Odessa, Ukraine, with approximately three hundred and fifty to four hundred Jewish immigrants making their way to Israel. We were within one day of reaching the Port of Haifa. As was customary, we gathered all of the Olim in the music lounge where they would receive a great deal of practical information concerning their arrival and debarkation procedures upon our arrival in Haifa.

It was also customary for the volunteers to serve them glasses of various juices and nice snacks. During our time together we would sing several songs to them in Hebrew and in Russian, ending with the Israeli national anthem, Hatikva. It was then that I always had the honor of sharing a message from the *Tanakh* (Old Testament) with them. It was always a message of hope and encouragement as they were about to begin a new life, in a new land, in a new culture and be exposed to a new language.

Since I was the only pastor on the team of volunteers I was always appointed this task which I accepted with gladness. The music salon where we gathered was a closed room, simply meaning that there were no windows that could be opened and no doors leading to the deck of the ship. The only doors were those leading to the interior steps and the elevators as well as the hallway of this particular floor.

I was a few minutes into my message from the Tanakh when I sensed that I was preaching with a special anointing. The thoughts and the words simply poured out of me. It is always such a wonderful thing for any preacher to experience the anointing of the Holy Spirit on them while preaching.

Probably 99.99% of the Jewish people I was ministering to that afternoon had never heard a message from the Word of God, but they were so kind and gracious none-the-less. They all sat there very quietly as I preached to them and my interpreter interpreted my words into the Russian language for their understanding.

I remember that I was sharing Isaiah 40:1 to help them understand that what they were doing in making their *aliyah* was God's plan for their lives and their children's future. Just as I was reading from that verse that says, *"Comfort, comfort my people, says your God. Speak tenderly to Jerusalem, and proclaim to her that her time of* exile *is over,"* was when it happened.

Keep in mind the room we were sitting in was closed to the outside of the ship's decks. There was no place the outside wind could enter the room and yet from the right side of the room I heard the sound of a mighty wind. As that wind passed over me I felt the hair on my arms stand straight up; I had goose bumps all over my body; my face and my arms tingled as if I had been shot full of Novocain. I felt an intense heat begin at the top of my head, and it ran all the way through my entire body to the soles of my feet.

The force of the wind was so strong I began to lose my footing, and I even stumbled backwards about two steps. I thought for a moment that I was going to fall to the floor. After I had regained my composure, I picked up with my message where I had left off just prior to this experience. But now something was different. I could feel it. I knew that I was now speaking with an even stronger and greater anointing than I had been speaking with before I felt the wind pass over me. It was truly a modern day "Upper Room" experience.

As I shared the Word of God with these precious people who had never heard it before, something quite miraculous happened. As I spoke the Word, suddenly from off to my left I heard someone shout in a very loud voice, *"Hallelujah, Hallelujah."* I was shocked beyond measure. What did I just hear? It was the universal word, "hallelujah," being shouted from a man who only spoke Russian and who had never heard a message from God's powerful Word before!

I continued to preach words of encouragement and hope to these wonderful children of God, and every time I quoted a Scripture and made a special point, I would hear from all over the room, *"Hallelujah, hallelujah."* I continued to preach, and they continued to shout, and many times they even *applauded* as they heard God's Word for the very first time. I began to think I was preaching in a

Pentecostal worship service. The more they shouted, the harder I preached. It was one of the most thrilling times of my thirty-three year ministry.

But let's stop to analyze this event for a moment. What had just happened? Well, the first thing I can tell you with no uncertainty is that what happened was not due to Barry Wagner. It was *not* me that caused such a reaction from these wonderful Jewish people as they heard the Word of God.

God made it very clear to me that what I had just witnessed was the *Power of His Word* reaching into the hearts of His people for the very first time! As His Word went forth it did so with the power of the Holy Spirit behind it. And because of the anointing that had fallen over me God's Word was penetrating the hearts and the spirits of these Jewish immigrants. You see, God was preparing them even before they arrived in Israel for the time that was just ahead of them to receive Him as *He* makes himself known to them in the land, just as He had promised He would do in Ezekiel 36:24-28. Praise His Holy Name forever!

"For I will take you out of the nations; I will gather you from all the countries and bring you back into your own land. I will sprinkle clean water on you, and you will be clean, I will cleanse you from all your impurities and from all your idols. I will give you a new heart and put a new spirit in you. I will remove from you your heart of stone and give you a heart of flesh. And I will put my Spirit in you and move you to follow my decrees and be careful to keep my laws. You will live in the land I gave your forefathers; you will be my people, and I will be your God."

What a powerful promise! The God of Abraham, Isaac and Jacob said *He* would do it. *He* will gather them from all the nations. *He* will bring them back into their own land— **Israel.** *He* will sprinkle clean water on them. *He* will give them a new heart. *He* will give them a new spirit. *He* will put His Spirit (the Holy Spirit) in them. *He* will teach them to follow His decrees. They will live in the land (*Israel*). They will be His people, and *He* will be their God!

And *He* is doing just that! Over one-and-a-half million Jewish people of the former Soviet Union countries alone and many thousands more from many other nations of the world have immigrated to Israel since the walls of Communism fell in 1989. God is truly a covenant keeper. He made a covenant with Abraham and the Israelites in Genesis 15:18-21, and it is being fulfilled in our lifetime. And if that isn't enough, He has asked Gentile believers to play a key role in what He is doing as He is restoring His people to their Promised Land! *What a wonderful honor and such an undeserved privilege!*

I can honestly say the three months I spent in Odessa, Ukraine, were the fastest three months of my life. Having completed my first two months in Ukraine, serving the Jewish people in their return to Israel from their Diaspora, I sensed that God was doing something in my spirit.

It was such an overwhelming feeling that this work I was doing would evolve into a lifelong calling. I knew that laboring in the *aliyah* would change my life completely, and not only my life, but Linda's life as well. I also knew it would be impossible for me to do what God was calling me to do without the full cooperation of the helpmate He had blessed my life with thirty-five years earlier. I understood that she would have to experience the same call on her life as I had.

I approached the base leadership with my request to have Linda fly to Odessa and work along side of me during my last month. Realizing that the Ebenezer Emergency Fund operated on a policy that the shortest time a volunteer could serve with them was for the entire three months, I really committed my request to prayer. I was certain that God would touch the hearts of the base leadership, and they would permit Linda to come.

I made my appeal to those who would have the final say in this matter and was told that they would all pray over my request and let me know their decision the next day.

Needless to say, I spent most of that night in prayer asking God to make a way where there seemed to be no way. After all, no one can do that task better than He can. I thought if He was able to change the course of the Red Sea for Moses and the children of Israel, He could certainly change the hearts of a few godly people.

When the next day arrived, I was called to the office for the leadership's decision. I was not too surprised to have them say to me, "It is fine for you to have Linda join you here for your last month of service. We know that God is doing something very special in your life, and we feel that she needs to be a part of it."

Within just a few days time I was at the Odessa Airport picking up the light of my life who was as excited about being there as I was to have her.

It was no time at all after Linda's arrival and her being a servant to God's chosen people that He placed the same call on her life as He had mine. Now we were of one mind, one heart, and one spirit.

Our last month in Odessa together—making three additional sailings to Israel with Jewish immigrants,—passed very quickly. It was now time to return to my pulpit at Trinity Assembly of God Church.

Since Linda and I had spent two months apart before her arrival in Odessa, I felt it would be good if we could spend some quality time together alone before stepping back into the demanding role of a pastor.

Our flight home would take us through Vienna, Austria. After discussing our plans together, we both agreed that it would be a wonderful opportunity to experience once again that beautiful country. This would be our third visit to Austria over the past twelve years. I have always said after our very first visit, if God ever created a more beautiful country than Austria, I have no idea where it might be.

So, it was decided. We would spend six days just driving around Austria, *but* we would make no prearranged plans concerning when and where we would go. We just prayed and asked God's Holy Spirit to direct our going out and our coming in. After our miraculous experience we both knew we could not have had a better tour guide than the Holy Spirit.

When we drove our rental car out of the Vienna Airport, we had no idea where we were headed; but once again God knew, and He had a specific itinerary already prepared for us.

It was amazing how everything fell so beautifully into place. The wonderful places God led us to for our shelter at night, the quant little villages with such warm and caring people, the excellent cafes and restaurants with tremendous food and great prices. Every single detail was orchestrated and planned out in advance by God. There was absolutely no doubt about it in our minds. God was in total control of this adventure.

One morning after waking I said to Linda, "Well, Sweetie, I wonder what special things God has planned for us today?" It wasn't too much later that we found out exactly what God had purposed in His heart for us during this trip.

Once again as usual, I started the car and just began to drive. I had no idea where I was headed. After about two hours of driving through the Austrian countryside we came to a beautiful little village called Mauthausen. It was such an inviting village with its narrow streets lined with interesting shops of all sorts. The smell of fresh baked bread and pastries was still hanging in the early morning air.

After spending some time going from shop to shop and sampling the wonderful apple strudel, we decided it was time to move on. As we backed from our parking space and headed out of the village I felt compelled to turn to the right onto a somewhat narrow country road. The road took us through a wooded area for a short distance and then into beautiful rolling hills with open fields on both sides of the road. As we continued driving, we suddenly noticed a large fortress-like structure ahead of us.

We had no idea that the road God put us on came to a dead end at the main gates of the Mauthausen Concentration Camp. In my ignorance I had never heard of Mauthausen, the village, or the camp. Until that day, I had no idea that there had been concentration camps in Austria during World War II. Of course, I knew of the many camps in Poland and Germany, but now suddenly we are sitting at the front gates of a place we will never forget as long as we live. It was a place that God had brought us to for His Divine purpose. God would soon use our visit to this hallowed place to deepen our call to the work of *aliyah*.

During our short stay in the village and even during the ride up to the camp the beautiful blue sky had been clear of clouds and the August sun warmed the morning hours making everything seem so perfect.

After parking the car we walked to the huge wooden gates that thousands of Jewish people and other prisoners had walked through to enter the camp from 1938 until the camp's liberation by the American forces on May 7, 1945. There was one very real difference between Linda and me and those thousands of prisoners who had passed through those very gates: Linda and I would be able to walk out of those gates alive and well.

It would be exactly three years and one week to the very day of Mauthausen's liberation that the state of Israel would be reborn as the Jewish homeland on May 14, 1948. Out of the ashes of the horrors of the Holocaust, God's people would once again have their own homeland after nearly two thousand years of being in exile.

We were both amazed at what happened next. Just as we walked through the gates the sky quickly turned dark and gray. It even began drizzling a fine misty rain leaving us with an overwhelming sense of heaviness.

As we passed through the gates we immediately entered the garage yard. This was a long and wide paved area with garage doors on either side where the Nazi officers' cars, motorcycles, and other vehicles had been housed. We would soon learn that it was on this very spot that thousands of prisoners were stripped naked and humiliated to begin their incoming process.

It was here at Mauthausen and its sub-camps that more than 195,000 Jews and other political prisoners were imprisoned. From that horrific number, over 105,000 men and women perished at the hands of the Nazis.

I made my way from the garage yard up several stone steps that put me on top of the ramparts—the walls that surrounded the camp. As I stood there on the wall, I was looking away from the camp, out across the beautiful rolling hillside with its lush, deep green fields. I noticed the little village of Mauthausen in the distance. The view was almost breathtaking, and it seemed so peaceful and serene.

I turned a mere one hundred and eighty degrees facing the opposite direction and found myself looking into what had become the bowels of hell for so many Jews. From that vantage point I could see the roofs of some of the wooden barracks that still remain. I could see the burial grounds where so many had been buried. I could see the chimneys of the cremation ovens that had once spewed out human ash allowing it to fall to the ground like the snows of winter.

The contrast was amazing. I stood there for some time wondering how many of God's precious children may have stood on this very spot and witnessed as I had the peace and beauty that the scenic view of the rolling hills had offered. And then, too, I couldn't help but wonder how many had turned in just the opposite direction only to look directly into the corridors of hell.

A short while later Linda and I were making our way through several other buildings of the camp. At one point we entered a long narrow room with tiled walls and stone tables. It was here that the executed prisoners were brought, laid on the tables and their gold teeth were knocked out of their mouths by waiting "dentists" with a small hammer and chisel just prior to their cremation or burial.

Entering the adjacent room we found ourselves standing in front of two cremation ovens. How many precious Jewish people had perished in those ovens? How many? Tears begin to fill my eyes and sorrow filled my spirit as I thought of the horror that was released here on the "Apple of God's eye."

Passing through a couple of narrow corridors we found ourselves standing in one of the infamous gas chambers. The chamber was camouflaged as a typical shower room. After the prisoners were ordered to strip themselves of all their clothing they were forced into the "shower room" still thinking they were going to be able to enjoy a much needed shower after the long grueling train ride in the infamous German box cars. After the doors were closed it was then that Cyclon B gas was released through the showerheads from an adjacent room. Thousands of Jews breathed their last breathe of life in this very room where Linda and I were now standing.

It was here that Linda said, "Barry, I have to get out of here. There is such a heavy spirit in here I can hardly breath. I have to get outside into the fresh air." I said, "Honey, you go ahead, but I can't leave just yet." After Linda left me standing there alone it was as if I could almost hear the screams and the wailing of the thousands of souls who perished there.

I began to cry, and then I began to sob uncontrollably. I had never experienced this kind of severe heartache and extreme pain in my innermost being before in my entire life. Something was happening to my inner man that was different and quite painful.

After Linda and I reunited, we continued to tour this camp of horror. We made our way into the "Wiener Graben" stone quarry just outside the rear gates of the camp. It was here that, on average, two thousand prisoners were forced to work every day cutting stones from the steep cliffs to be used in the construction of other buildings at the camp and throughout Austria. This was also a place of execution where several thousand prisoners were shot or crushed to death by falling rocks.

We stood at the top of "Parachutists' Cliff." This was at the very top of the stone quarry with a several hundred-foot drop to the quarry floor. It was here that SS guards would push prisoners over the side to their death just for sport. Entire groups of Dutch Jews were killed in this manner.

Just prior to re-entering the gate to the main compound of the camp I noticed a very prominent statue of a man. I approached it with great interest. As I read the inscription affixed at the base I learned that it was a statue of Soviet Army General Karbyshev. During the freezing night of February 16, 1945, General Karbyshev along with an additional two hundred prisoners were stripped naked and forced to stand in front of the wall of the camp while ice-cold water was poured over them until their bodies were frozen.

How is it even possible for one "human" being to perpetrate such horror on another human? This was *pure evil* released in its rawest form!

As we made our way back through the open gate with an extremely heavy spirit hanging over us, we made one last stop. It was in one of the prisoners' barracks—Barrack Number Six. The small narrow wooden bunk beds are still there. Each of the beds had to be shared by no less than two prisoners, but many times it was as many as four starving, emaciated bodies. There were no mattresses on the beds. The prisoners simply slept on the hard wooden structures.

At the far end of the barracks we noticed a small wooden podium. As we approached the podium we saw what appeared to be a guest book. It was placed there to give visitors an opportunity to put their feelings into writing. We leafed through the book looking for entries written in English.

We began reading the many heart-felt sentiments of past visitors. As both Linda and I were reading the same entry, our eyes fell upon the writer's last sentence at the same time. The writer said this: "After seeing this place of horror I have but one question—*why*?" It was as if our eyes had been glued to the writer's last word, *why*? I looked at Linda as she looked at me, and we began to cry almost uncontrollably. Something happened to us both at that instant, and we knew without any doubt whatsoever that we would have to commit the rest of our lives to helping the Jews of the Diaspora in their return to their homeland.

Now we understood perfectly why God so miraculously directed our steps to Mauthausen. It was to prepare our hearts for the work that would lie ahead of us.

After being reunited with my wonderful congregation and settling back into my regular pastoral duties at the church I could not shake the fact that I was feeling like a fish out of water. I was still not totally certain where God was leading me. I would go to my office every morning, lie flat on my face in front of my desk, and cry out to God to give me a clear understanding of what it was He wanted me to do among the Jewish people.

It was the second week of September, 1998, when Linda and I returned to the church from Odessa. It wasn't until the latter part of November that God gave me total clarity of the new calling and the new anointing he had placed on my life.

The finality of the call on our lives came from Heaven's Throne Room by way of an extremely emotional dream.

Chapter Twelve

A Life-Changing Dream

Many times God's voice can be heard in the awesome beauty of nature. Perhaps, in His handiwork of creation as a warm summer breeze blows gently through the trees; in the sound of a rippling mountain stream, or in a beautiful red and orange sky as the sun sets quickly in the west. His voice may be heard as one looks at the beautiful snow-covered mountain peaks of a nearby mountain range.

God speaks of this truth in Romans 1:20: *"For since the creation of the world God's invisible qualities—His eternal power and Divine nature—have been clearly seen, being understood from what has been made, so that men are without excuse."*

Many times God reaches the heart of those who diligently seek Him through that "still small voice" heard deep within the human soul. Suddenly, a deep sense of peace floods over us, and we just know that we know we have heard from the heart of God, and the matter we have been dealing with has been settled.

For others, God speaks many times through dreams and visions. *"And afterward, I will pour out my Spirit on all people. Your sons and daughters will prophesy, your old men will dream dreams, your young men will see visions"* (Joel 2:28). And so it was for me when God used a dream to finalize His call on my life, to leave my position as a senior pastor and become involved full-time in the return of the Jewish people to Israel.

Prior to our leaving Trinity Assembly of God Church, God paid a divine visit to me one night by way of a dream to redirect our ministry and to change our calling.

On this eventful night I had gone to bed as usual and had slipped into a deep, peaceful sleep. Then it began—a dream that would change my life forever.

I saw a large rectangular room that was void of any furnishings. There were three doors in the room, one on the northern wall, one on the southern wall, and one on the western wall. It was clear to me that I was on the outside of the door on the southern wall. As I opened the door and gazed into the room I was horrified by what I saw. There in the center of the room was the largest serpent that I had ever seen. I immediately recognized this frightening creature as an anaconda. This is the world's largest snake and is found in the jungles and waterways of South America. The anaconda many times grows to twenty-nine feet in length and can weigh as much as five hundred and fifty pounds; however, this was no ordinary anaconda. The size of this serpent was far beyond anything that has ever been known to exist.

I noticed that most of the serpent's body was coiled up in the center of the room with part of its body stretched out across the floor running toward the wall on the west side of the room. Its body continued to go up the wall and across the ceiling until its head was immediately over the rest of its coiled body lying on the floor. Suddenly the door on the northern wall flew open, and two small boys entered the room. Somehow I knew that they were brothers, and God even revealed their ages to me. The eldest was four years old and his brother was two. I saw the two-year-old walk to the coiled up body of the serpent and climb into the center of the coils. The four-year-old also walked over to the serpent and simply leaned against its over sized body.

Having watched the two young boys enter the room with great interest, the serpent began to move its head at the ceiling level in a threatening manner. I knew then that these two precious little lives were hanging in the balance.

Since the boys did not realize what this creature was and were totally unaware of the danger they were in, I knew I had to warn them. I began screaming to them as loudly as I could from the doorway where I was standing. I cried out, "Go back, go back; you're in great danger. You will be killed." The serpent became even more aroused, and I could see that it was about to make its deadly strike on the boys. I screamed even louder, "Please, go back; go back. You will be killed," but the boys were paying no attention to me in the least. It was as if I was speaking a foreign language to them, and I was, as I would find out just minutes later.

During all the confusion that was taking place, my attention was drawn to the door entering the room from the west. The door never opened, but I knew that my youngest son Bryan was in the room behind that door. I screamed out to him, "Bryan, don't come in. There is great danger here, and you will be killed. Stay where you are." He took my warning and remained in safety behind the door to the west.

It was then that I realized that if *I* didn't do something more than simply cry out warnings, these two beautiful children would surely perish. I did the only thing I knew to do. I ran into the room with the serpent and the two boys. I first reached into the coiled body of the serpent and picked up the two-year-old boy in my left arm. I then reached down and picked up the four-year-old in my right arm. As I began to turn to make our exit to the door of safety on the southern wall, I noticed something that startled me so badly that I could hardly move. As I looked down at the top of the heads of these two precious children I saw that they were both wearing *kippahs* (Jewish skull caps). These boys were two of God's chosen people. After recovering from my moment of shock, I ran as quickly as I could with the two boys in my arms toward the door of safety on the southern wall.

Passing through the door and slamming it shut behind us I knew that these children were safe and would be able to live out their lives in safety. At that moment God woke me from this unsettling dream. Immediately, I began to question God as to what the dream meant.

God Interprets His Own Dream

God's interpretation came quickly. He said, "Barry, the serpent was Satan himself—the mortal enemy of the Jewish people—who from the beginning of time has tried everything in his power to destroy my people.

"The two Jewish boys represented all of my chosen people, the Seed of Abraham. The door on the northern wall represented the 'Land of the North'—Russia and all of the former Soviet Union countries.

"The door on the southern wall represented Israel, which lies due south of the former Soviet Union. This is where you took my children to safety. The reason you saw yourself in this dream is because I am calling you to *go* into the former Soviet Union countries to help bring my children home to the land of their inheritance, the land of Israel."

I then asked God, "But what did it mean when I realized my son was safe behind the door on the western wall?" And then God spoke these words into my spirit so clearly. "Barry, I was showing you that your beloved son was living in safety in the land of the West (America) while my sons and my daughters are living in grave danger in the land of the *North* (Russia)."

As I heard these things coming from the very heart of Abba (Father) I was so shaken in my spirit that I sat straight up in my bed and began to cry uncontrollably. It was then that I realized what I must do. I knew without any doubt in my mind that I would have to resign from the church and leave the wonderful people we had come to love so much over the past six years. I would have to step out on faith and become involved full-time in aiding the Jewish people of the former Soviet Union countries in their return to the land of Israel.

Do you remember what we spoke about in chapter two of this book concerning *revelation?* We concluded that with every new revelation which God gives us comes responsibility. Through the dream that I had just experienced, God gave me new revelation, and now I had to be willing to accept the full extent of the responsibility that came along with it.

Linda and I both knew that it would now be necessary for us to resign our position at the church and step out into the unknown with nothing but a new call of God on our lives and a bucket full of faith.

It wasn't until now that I fully understood why it was so important for God to take us through our three-and-a-half-year wilderness experience. He had to bring us to the point where we could trust fully in Him and to know completely that He would provide for all of our needs.

I called for a board meeting the first day of December and tendered my resignation effective the first Sunday of January, 1999.

After announcing our resignation to the congregation, it was amazing to both Linda and me to have several of our people tell us that they had known for some time that I would not be their pastor much longer after my return from Ukraine. God had already prepared them for this transition, just as He was now preparing us.

As Linda and I prayed for God's leading during those months leading up to December, we both heard over and over again the word *"Educate."* God was calling us to take the message of the return of the Jews to Israel to the Body of Christ and to educate believers around the world as to what

God was doing in these last days with His people and the land of Israel. It was that understanding that motivated us to call for the special board meeting where I would tender my resignation.

It wasn't too much later that the stark reality of our decision hit us squarely between the eyes. *Oh boy, here we go again Lord!* No money in the bank; we would be required to move out of the parsonage; there would be no more pay checks, no more utilities being paid by the church, no more medical insurance, no social security being paid, etc., etc.

As unsettling as those realizations were, I continued to maintain a wonderful sense of peace deep within my spirit. It truly was that *"peace that passes all human understanding."* Do you remember how God had prepared Linda and me for this moment in our lives? Our all-knowing God knew that this day would eventually come. He also knew what He would require of us, and we had to be prepared for it. That's right. The three-and-a-half years of our *"Wilderness Journey."* It was all part of God preparing us to be able to step out on nothing but faith when that day finally arrived. This was our final exam. Graduation day was here. Would we pass this test, or would we fail?

I feel very deeply that we did pass God's final exam the night of the board meeting when I tendered my resignation, realizing even then that we had absolutely no resources of our own to sustain us in our new calling. But please understand, it wasn't anything we did, it was what God did for us during those important years of preparation. As painful as those days were, Linda and I both realized that if we had not experienced what God had brought us through, we would never have been able to walk away from everything as we did. He had to bring us to that point of total brokenness and to being able to trust totally in Him for our every need.

Chapter Thirteen

From Pastor to a
Jeremiah Fisherman

"But now I will send for many fishermen,"
declares the Lord, "and they will catch them."
Jeremiah 16:16a

These prophetic words written two thousand seven hundred years ago by the prophet Jeremiah are words that were concealed from my understanding until the appointed time.

I had read this Scripture as well as hundreds of other prophetic Scriptures for twenty-five years of my preaching ministry. I preached them, I taught them, I did everything with them except understand them.

When God's appointed time had finally arrived it was as if spiritual scales had fallen from my eyes when I read those same Scriptures once again. If God had revealed the prophetic Scriptures that speak of the Jews returning to Israel from all the nations twenty years earlier I could not have done anything with that revelation. The walls of Communism had not yet come down and the Jews were not able to flee from the former Soviet Union countries.

Everything happens according to God's perfect time table, and this was no exception. I want to encourage you with this great truth. If you are praying for a special need in your life—perhaps for salvation of a loved one, for a financial reversal, spiritual or physical healing, that new job, or perhaps for that special someone to spend the rest of your life with—KEEP PRAYING! Wait on the Lord with total trust and confidence in knowing that God has your very best interest at heart. He and He alone knows what is best for you and when it should take place in your life. I can assure you that it will come to pass according to God's perfect time table—not *yours!* Always remember that God's delays are not God's denials.

When the time had finally arrived for us to step out into our new calling, God brought Mel Hoelzle, President and Founder of Ezra International, into our lives in a most miraculous way.

At the time of God's initial call on my life for the work of *aliyah* I had no idea that Ezra International even existed, but God did, and He had a plan.

It was on a Monday night in 1998. Mel was meeting with the Ezra International Board at his home in Seattle, Washington. At that time a husband and wife team had been working with Ezra. From time to time they would travel to the U.S. from Kiev, Ukraine, to speak in churches to help in the fund-raising process. Due to some personal issues and health concerns, however, the Ezra Board found it necessary to release this couple from their work.

Of course this was of major concern for the board since this couple were the only people who were out speaking on behalf of the ministry of Ezra International.

As the Board shared their thoughts and ideas together they turned the need completely over to the Lord in prayer. Just a short while later a word of knowledge was given to one of the board members which he promptly shared with the rest of the board.

The word that was given from the Lord was this: *"I am about to send you a man."*

Meanwhile, back in Florida I was speaking at a monthly meeting of pastors, missionaries, evangelists and leaders of various ministries. Prior to getting up to speak, the Bishop of the organization handed me a piece of paper with a phone number and a man's name on it. He said that I was to call this man because he had money to help in the return of Jews to Israel.

Upon arrival at my home, I immediately picked up the phone and dialed the number which had been given to me.

A man answered on the other end, "Hello, Hoelzle residence." It was Mel, the man who God would soon use to change my life and my ministry forever. After identifying myself I began to share my heart with Mel concerning my love for the Jewish people and what I felt God was calling me to do. He was calling me to take the message of Israel's "Final Return" to the Body of Christ. I also shared the dream that God had given me to finalize this call.

At the same time I was speaking into Mel's ear the Holy Spirit was speaking into his spirit, "Mel, this is the man I said I would send."

After more discussion and the shedding of a few tears I was told that the board would come to Orlando to meet with Linda and me for a face to face interview.

Our time together with Mel and the Ezra Board took place on December 30 and 31, 1998. After two days of sharing our hearts with the board and much prayer, it was decided that this was truly a "divine appointment." I would become Ezra International's first U.S. Representative.

At one point during our meeting, Linda and I had to dismiss ourselves. We received a phone call from our youngest son telling us that our daughter-in-law was about to give birth to our third grandchild at a nearby Orlando hospital. What a day! God not only confirmed His perfect will for our lives and ministry, but He gave us a beautiful grandson, Bryan Christopher, as well.

My first order of business with Ezra International was to travel to Kiev, Ukraine, with Mel. It was his plan for us to travel by train across the country appointing representatives to work with us in the various regions.

A person has not truly lived until they have spent several days and nights on a Russian train. The trip was interesting to say the least. Mel and I were accompanied on that first trip by Viktor Mykhaylov, who was serving Ezra as the head of the Kiev office as well as being responsible for the Ezra work throughout the entire former Soviet Union countries.

Also traveling with us was Ira Friedman, who was a Jewish immigrant herself from eastern Ukraine, close to the Russian border. She and her family had made their *aliyah* to Israel seven years earlier and were now living in Karmiel, Israel. She volunteered to be part of the team since she was familiar with Ukraine. We were so thankful for her much-needed assistance.

God made it very clear to both Mel and me at the outset of our journey that He was at the very core of this ministry. Without fail, at every stop we made we learned that God had already gone before us. He had already called the people He wanted to use in this Holy work. It happened with them just as it had with me. They, too, had no idea that there was an organization called Ezra International, but God did.

One of those persons God led us to on this cross-country trip was a truck driver from the city of Mariupol, a city situated on the coast of the Sea of Azov in southeastern Ukraine. His name was Vladimir Gusyev, a Christian believer who loves God with all of his heart. God had laid it on Vladimir's heart about two years earlier that he was to assist the Jewish people of his city to return to Israel, but he had no financial means to help.

God had spoken to Vladimir and said that he would make contact with a business man who had money to help

Jewish people immigrate to Israel. Vladimir was not quite clear as to what God was telling him, so he did what he *thought* God was saying. He began to go from business owner to business owner throughout his city telling them that they were to give him money to help Jewish people go to Israel. Needless to say, the response he received from the business owners was not the response he had expected.

It was shortly after that experience that God's perfect plan began to unfold. It started the evening that Mel, the other two members of our team, and I arrived in Mariupol by train.

After spending several hours with Vladimir and seeking God's direction through prayer, we all knew that he would be one of Ezra's first representatives in Ukraine. This man of God served Ezra International and the Jewish people so well that he was later promoted to the Kiev office where he handled all of the finances for the entire FSU work and was responsible for all of Ezra's work throughout Ukraine.

Recently God called Vladimir and his lovely wife, Nadiya to become pastors of a thriving church in Kiev. From his new position as pastor, Vladimir is able to educate his church, other pastors, and other congregations about what God is doing with the Jewish people. So his work in the *aliyah* continues, just from a different platform.

What happened with Vladimir was played out in just the same way time after time wherever our team went throughout Ukraine. God had already gone before us. He had already placed His call on each person's life, and they were just waiting for the appointed time. That appointed time happened as Mel and his team arrived in their city, and God brought us miraculously together.

Nearly every representative we put into position on that trip in 1999 continues to labor with Ezra in the work of *aliyah*. Through their efforts and the efforts of the fishermen who are working with them, Ezra International has been able to assist over sixty-five thousand Jewish people from ten former Soviet Union countries to return to Israel in fulfillment of Bible prophecy. Ezra is presently assisting an additional thirty-one thousand to make their *aliyah*.

Since those early days in January of 1999, Ezra International now has representatives and Jeremiah 16:16 fishermen in ten former Soviet Union countries as well as throughout Latin America. The home office in the FSU continues to be situated in Kiev, Ukraine, where a full-time staff of fourteen fully committed believers is being used of God to fulfill Bible prophecy.

But why do they do it? Why do they give themselves so tirelessly to do this holy work? Why do the Jeremiah 16:16 fishers labor with Ezra International in the waste lands of Siberia, many times going on foot through the sub-zero cold, the snow and ice to locate the forgotten Jewish people in their regions? Why did God call Mel and his lovely wife, Joanne, to begin the ministry of Ezra International? Why did God call Linda and me from our church in Chuluota, Florida, to be a part of this work?

There is one simple answer to each one of those questions. It is simply because the *aliyah* is God's eternal plan for them and the land of Israel, and He is calling Gentile believers to labor with Him in their "Final Return." God is in the final process of rebuilding physical Israel as well as rebuilding spiritual Israel, just as He said He would do throughout the writings of the prophets.

The *aliyah* is not Ezra International's plan for the Jewish people of the world. It is not the plan of the International Christian Embassy Jerusalem. It is not Bridges for Peace's plan. It is not Ebenezer Emergency Funds' plan. It is no organization's plan, nor is it any person's plan. It is, in fact, God's plan and His alone.

It is His plan to gather the Jewish people from the four corners of the globe and bring them home to Eretz Israel. I can assure you that this prophecy continues to be fulfilled with every passing day, and it will continue to take place until He says, "It is finished."

But is there Scriptural proof of this claim? Does God really speak of the "Final Return" in His Word? Let's look together in the following chapter to see what God is truly saying about this end-time world wide event.

Part 3

God's Plan
for the Jews
and the Church

Chapter Fourteen

Scripture Confirms the "Final Return"

*"For I will take you out of the nations;
I will gather you from all the countries and
bring you back into your own land."*
Ezekiel 36:24

Throughout my twenty-five years of preaching I always told my congregations not to accept everything I said from the pulpit at face value. I would instruct them to go to the Word of God to confirm whatever I shared with them in the form of a sermon or a teaching. I instructed them to throw out anything that could not be supported by Scripture. The Word of God must always be the final authority of everything we preach and teach.

So it is with the "Final Return" of the Jewish people. If this event cannot be confirmed and supported by the Word of God then it is not of God, and we should have nothing to do with it. However, that is not the case.

It is my intention throughout this chapter to present sufficient Scriptural evidence to help us all know without any doubt whatsoever that what we are witnessing in the Jewish immigration to Israel is, in fact, God's plan.

It has recently been estimated that there are over two hundred and fifty plus Scriptures in the *Tanakh* (the Old Testament) alone that speak about the Jewish people returning to Israel in the last days.

I tell congregations wherever I speak that if the *aliyah* is so important to God that He chose to speak of it over two hundred and fifty times in His Word, then it seems natural that it should be that important to each of us as well. If it is that important to Abba, it should be something that demands our immediate attention.

Of course time and space will not permit us to examine all two hundred and fifty plus Scriptures, but we can look very closely at several of them to confirm what God is doing with His people and Israel during this prophetic season in which we live.

After I returned from spending three months in Odessa assisting several thousand Jewish people in their return to Israel, I cried out to God in prayer every day. I prayed, "Oh God, please show me your heart. Please reveal to me that thing which is at the center of your heart at this moment of human history." God used His Word to show me and to confirm to my spirit once and for all that the return of the Jewish people was that thing which was at the very depth of His heart.

For nearly two thousand years—since the destruction of the Holy Temple and the city of Jerusalem—the Jews have been scattered throughout the world in the Diaspora. Now is the time that God is calling them home to the land of their inheritance, the land of Israel.

God, through His Holy Spirit, inspired each of the prophets, both major prophets and the minor prophets, to speak of the event that we now see taking place during our lifetime. The Scriptures which we are about to look at were written more than two thousand seven hundred years ago, and now they are being fulfilled before our very eyes. What exciting days we are blessed to be living in!

As I sought after God's heart and His plans, He began my time of revelation concerning the *aliyah* with Amos 3:7, which teaches us, *"Surely the Sovereign Lord does nothing without revealing His plan to His servants the prophets."*

Please take notice that God did not say He would reveal His plans first to the preacher or the evangelist or the teacher BUT he would reveal His plans to the prophets. Which prophets is God referring to? Exactly, He is referring to the Jewish prophets of the Tanakh.

I really didn't have to be a Philadelphia lawyer to understand that if I wanted to know God's prophetic plans for Israel and the Jewish people of the Diaspora I would have to look to the writings of the Jewish prophets.

Let's look at just a few Scriptures penned by the prophet Isaiah.

*"And He shall set up an ensign for the nations, and shall assemble the outcasts of Israel, and gather together the dispersed of Judah from the **four corners of the earth**"* (Isaiah 11:12 KJV, emphasis mine).

*"But thou, Israel, art my servant, Jacob whom I have chosen, the seed of Abraham my friend. Thou who I have taken **from the ends of the earth**, and called thee from the chief men thereof, and said unto thee, Thou art my servant; I have chosen thee, **and not cast thee away**"* (Isaiah 41:8,9 KJV).

Still today there are those who cling to the false doctrine of Replacement Theology which teaches that God has turned His back on Israel, He has rejected them, and He has broken His covenant with them. The Bible in the above verse and several others that we will be looking at makes it very clear that He has *not* nor will He *ever* reject Israel, but more of that later.

Wow, look at this verse!

*"Do not be afraid, for I am with you; I will bring your children from the **east** and gather you from the **west**, I will say to the **north**, 'Give them up!' and to the **south**, 'Do not*

hold them back.' Bring my sons from afar and my daughters from the ends of the earth—everyone who is called by my name, whom I created for my glory, whom I formed and made. Lead out those who have eyes but are blind, who have ears but are deaf" (Isaiah 43:5-8).

Let's see what Jeremiah has to say about this God-ordained world event.

"However, the days are coming," declares the Lord, *"when men will no longer say, 'As surely as the Lord lives, who brought the Israelites up out of Egypt,' but they will say, 'As surely as the Lord lives, who brought the Israelites up out of the land of the north and out of all the countries where He had banished them.' For I will restore them to the land I gave their forefathers"* (Jeremiah 16:14, 15).

Jeremiah continues in chapter 28:14, *"I will be found by you,"* declares the Lord, *"and will bring you back from captivity. I will gather you from all the nations and places where I have banished you,"* declares the Lord, *"and will bring you back to **the place from which I carried you into exile**"* (emphasis mine).

As I had mentioned in a previous chapter it was so hard for me to believe that the true meaning of these Scriptures had been hidden for so long. How did I miss it? After the spiritual scales had fallen from my eyes it became so very clear. I felt as the blind man did when he shouted, "I was blind, but now I see!" Thank God for new revelation.

Jeremiah had much to say about this prophetic event. Take a look at this one from Jeremiah 31:7-10.

*This is what the Lord says: "Sing with joy for Jacob; shout for the foremost of the nations. Make your praises heard, and say, O Lord, save your people, the remnant of Israel. See, I will bring them from the land of the north and gather them from the ends of the earth. Among them will be the blind and the lame, expectant mothers and **women in labor**; a great throng will return. They will come with weeping; they will pray as I bring them back. I will lead them beside* *streams of water on a level path where they will not stumble, because I am Israel's father, and Ephraim is my first born son. Hear the word of the Lord, O nations; proclaim it in distant coastlands; He who scattered Israel will gather them and will watch over His flock like a shepherd"* (emphasis mine).

Jeremiah speaks of the fact that even *women in labor* will return. Allow me to share with you an extremely blessed event which took place on one of the flights to Israel with a plane load of Jewish immigrants. Our Ezra staff in Ukraine shared this account with us.

When the flight took off from Borispol International Airport in Kiev, there were 268 passengers on board. When the plane arrived in Tel Aviv there were 269 passengers on board.

What happened? Did the flight make a stop en route to pick up one additional passenger? No, that's not what happened. The fact of the matter is that one of the expectant mothers gave birth to a beautiful baby girl while in flight. Praise the Lord! He declared through the prophet Jeremiah that even expectant mothers would return. This was truly Bible prophecy being fulfilled.

That new baby girl—like all the others on that flight—became an Israeli citizen the moment she arrived in Tel Aviv, Israel. God is so faithful to fulfill what He said He would do throughout His prophetic word.

Now let's see what Ezekiel has to tell us about the *aliyah*. He writes in his prophetic book:

*This is what the Sovereign Lord says: "When I gather the people of Israel from the nations where they have been scattered, I will show myself holy among them in the sight of the nations. Then they will live in **their own land**, which I gave to my servant Jacob"* (Ezekiel 28:25, emphasis mine).

He continues his thoughts in the next verse:

"They will live there in safety and will build houses and plant vineyards; they will live in safety when I inflict punishment on all their neighbors who maligned them.

Then they will know that I am the lord their God" (Ezekiel 28:26).

Many have asked me, "Why is God bringing the Seed of Abraham back to Israel?" God does a very fine job of answering that question Himself as He anointed Ezekiel to write these words:

"Therefore say to the house of Israel, 'This is what the Sovereign Lord says; It is not for your sake, O house of Israel, 'that I am going to do these things, but for the sake of my holy name" (Ezekiel 36:22a).

What do you suppose God is referring to here, when He says He is going to do these things for the sake of His Holy name? He speaks more of this in verse 23:

*"I will show the **holiness of my great name**, which has been profaned among the nations, the name you have profaned among them. Then the nations will know that I am the Lord, when I show myself holy through you before their eyes."*

I believe that God is referring directly back to the covenant He had made with Abram in Genesis 13:15 when He told Abram, *"All the land that you see I will give to you and your offspring **forever**."* God used a very important word here. A word that is often times overlooked.

He told Abram, the father of the Israelites, that the land would be theirs *forever!* I tell congregations that you don't have to be a rocket scientist to figure this one out. I am just a simple guy from Pennsylvania Dutch (Amish) background, and even I get it. When God says forever, He means *forever!* Not for an extended period of time, not for a season, not for just awhile, but *forever!*

But what land is God speaking about here in Genesis 13:15? Can we be fully certain what plot of real estate He is telling Abram is part of His eternal covenant with him?

Let's look at Genesis 15:18-21 to see if we can pinpoint the land that God is referring to.

"On that day the Lord made a covenant with Abram and said, 'To your descendants I give this land, from the river of Egypt to the great river, the Euphrates, the land of the Kenites, Kenizzites, Kadmonites, Hittites, Perizzites, Rephaites, Amorites, Canaanites, Girgashites and Jebusites.'"

What we are reading about here are the *original* Biblical borders of Israel. A covenant land for the homeland of the Jewish people given to them by God Himself as His gift to them *forever!*

Wherever I speak I tell congregations that the Israel of today is not the Israel of the Bible. Suddenly there is a deafening holy hush that falls over the auditorium, and I can almost hear my own heart beat. The people are probably wondering at that point what planet this man is from.

I then finish my thought, "Israel of today is not the Israel of the Bible. It is part of it." You see, God gave us the original Biblical borders here in Genesis 15:18-21. The River of Egypt which flows into the Mediterranean Sea just south of Gaza was the Southern most boarder of Israel. Then God says that the land would extend to the *"great river, the Euphrates."* We all know where that is, don't we? The Euphrates River flows right through the country of Iraq and through the center of Baghdad or ancient Babylon. So now we have the Southern and the Eastern borders of the land of Israel. Of course the western boarder of Israel is the shores of the Mediterranean Sea.

Now, when you add in the lands of the Kenites, the Kenizzites, the Kadmonites, the Hittites and all the other "ites" we can have a complete picture of the land God gave to the Israelites through the covenant He made with Abram.

The true "Promised Land" takes in a very small part of Egypt, all of modern day Israel, part of Jordan, part of Iraq, part of Syria, and Lebanon.

Here is the problem as it exists today concerning the land of Israel. God promised in His covenant with Abram *all* of the land mentioned above, but at present Israel is in control of only what we know as modern-day Israel—a very small portion of the land that God had originally promised them.

Remember, God said He gave that land to the Israelites as an inheritance *forever.* Now either God meant forever when He said it, or He lied to Abram. If there is one thing I know for certain, God is not a liar.

That being the case, it seems to me that God must return *all* of this land to Israel in order to keep His promise and the covenant He made with Abram back in Genesis 15. How will this land be returned to Israel? Many believe it will happen through a great Arab/Israeli war that seems to be looming on the horizon. Iran's goal is to wipe Israel off the map. Syria has been saber-rattling for several years now as they are demanding the return of the Golan Heights to them.

Once again, as in the past, Israel will be attacked on at least three or four fronts by its Arab neighbors. Their goal will be the complete destruction of Israel. Also, let's not forget that Israel created a hostile land within its own borders when they turned the Gaza strip over to the Palestinians.

This is why God said in Ezekiel 36:22 that the reason He would bring the Jewish people home to their own land was not for the sake of the House of Israel but for the sake of His Holy Name. He made a promise and a covenant, and now He must keep His Word. God said that after the Jews are back in the land of their inheritance and He accomplishes all these things, *"Then the nations will know that I am the Lord,"* declares the Sovereign Lord, *"when I show myself holy through you before their eyes"* (Ezekiel 36:23b).

God is bringing the Seed of Abraham back into their own land to keep His word, thus protecting His Holy Name, as well as for the purpose of rebuilding physical Israel and spiritual Israel. We will address the rebuilding of spiritual Israel in a later chapter.

Here is but another of the many Scriptures of the Old Testament that speaks of God gathering His people from all the nations:

*"For I will take you out of the nations; I will gather you from **all the countries** and bring you back into your own land. I will sprinkle clean water on you and you will be clean; I will cleanse you from all your impurities and from all your idols. I will give you a new heart and put a new spirit in you; I will remove your heart of stone and give you a heart of flesh. And I will put my spirit in you and move you to follow my decrees and be careful to keep my laws. **You will live in the land I gave your forefathers;** you will be my people, and I will be your God"* (Ezekiel 36:24-28, Emphasis mine).

If you have a real love for the Jewish people and for the land of Israel but these next Scriptures don't move you to shouting "Praise the Lord," I don't know what will. God is waiting so patiently to pour out His richest blessings on Israel and its people, and He will. This is really something very powerful, wonderful and exciting.

*"Therefore this is what the Sovereign Lord says: I will now bring Jacob [Israel] back from captivity and will have compassion on all the people of Israel, and I will be zealous for my holy name. They will forget their shame and all the unfaithfulness they showed toward me when they lived in safety in their land with no one to make them afraid. When I have brought them back from the nations and have gathered them from the countries of their enemies, I will show myself holy through them in the sight of many nations. Then they will know that I am the Lord their God, for though I sent them into exile among the nations, [70 A.D.], **I will gather them to their own land, not leaving any behind.** I will no longer hide my face from them, for **I will pour out my Spirit on the house of Israel,** declares the Sovereign Lord"* (Ezekiel 39:25-29, emphasis mine).

There are so many other powerful and equally exciting Scriptures recorded in the writings of the prophets that time and space do not permit me to share. Even with just the sampling of such Scriptures we have shared together it is impossible to miss what God is saying to us all. He said He would gather His people out of the nations and return them to their own land, and He is doing just that. These prophecies are being fulfilled before our eyes, and yet so much of the Body of Christ is not even aware that it is taking place.

The very thing that is closest to the heart of Abba is taking place right now—on our watch—and unfortunately so much of the Body is still unaware. I can only pray that what is written in the pages of this book might serve as a wake-up call to the Church that God so badly wants to use and bless as we work together in partnership with Him to richly bless His people in their return to their "Promised Land."

Once again we are reminded of Genesis 12:3:

"I will bless those who bless you and those who curse you I will curse; and all peoples on the earth will be blessed through you."

I firmly believe that if every church, every pastor, every denomination and every believer would just allow the above scripture to get deep down into their spirits, and if they would claim it for their own, they would see miraculous positive changes take place in their lives and in their churches— changes that they never thought possible.

How do I know that this promise of God is still operational in our day? Because I have experienced it.

When I left my church in 1998 for three months to serve the Jewish people in Ukraine I had been wearing eyeglasses for over thirty years. In fact, they were bifocals, since I needed them for reading and distance.

Every morning I would take them off the night stand, place them on my face, wear them all day long, and return them to the night stand before lying down for the night. This was my routine for over thirty years.

I was seven weeks into my time in Odessa when something miraculous happened that I didn't ask for or pray for. It just happened. That particular day I woke up and placed my glasses on my face as usual, but I noticed that everything seemed quite blurry. This is strange, I thought, so I took the glasses off, and I never put them back on the entire time I was in Ukraine.

God had chosen to completely heal my eyes. Why did He do it? I never even thought to ask for this healing, and yet it came anyway. But why? For over seven years from that day forward I enjoyed perfect vision. No glasses, no contacts, no corrective lenses of any kind.

I firmly believe it was God's way of blessing me as I was being a blessing to His chosen people. I was simply loving them with the unconditional love of Christ. I was being a servant to them. I was holding them in my arms, crying tears down their backs as they cried tears down my back. I was treating the "Apple of His Eye" with dignity and respect. This was something most of them had never experienced in their entire lives.

Why did this wonderful miracle happen? Because God promised us that if we will simply be a blessing to His people, He would bless us (Genesis 12:3).

Chapter Fifteen

God's Calling to the Church

This is what the Sovereign Lord says:
"See, I will beckon to the Gentiles, I will lift up
my banner to the peoples; they will bring your
sons in their arms and carry your
daughters on their shoulders."
Isaiah 49:22

The three months I served in Odessa, Ukraine, being a servant to the precious Jewish people were very rewarding days for me personally; yet at the same time they were also extremely emotional days.

Everyday for three solid months I was going in and out of the apartments, the homes and the farm houses of the Jewish people who we were assisting with their *aliyah*. Everyday, I witnessed the stark poverty, the lack of running water, the absence of electricity, the missing toilets, the hungry elderly, and children with inadequate clothing.

I saw so much that most Americans have only perhaps read about. I smelled the wide range of odors in home after home that confirmed the presence of poverty.

With the many sights and smells still very fresh in my mind after my arrival home, God used them to drive me to my knees in prayer for our Jewish brothers and sisters scattered throughout the former Soviet Union countries and around the world.

Every day I would lie flat on my face before God and enter into a time of intercession for these precious people of God. I would cry out to Him, "Oh God, you have shown me that it is your perfect will and your perfect plan for the Jews of the Diaspora to return to the land of their inheritance. But God, they are so poor. They are having trouble buying a sixteen-cent loaf of bread for their dinner table. How can they afford to make such a move to a new country? Who will help them in their time of desperation?"

Day after day I would cry out this same prayer to God with my prayers seemingly falling on deaf ears. And once again I had to remind myself that God's delays are not God's denials. Then one day at His appointed time, His answer came suddenly to my spirit as the Holy Spirit directed me to the Word of God.

The Holy Spirit of God sent me to Isaiah 49:22 and said so clearly, "Barry, here is the answer you were looking for."

Dear Body of Christ, please, if you have missed everything else I have shared with you up to this point, I beg of you, **please do not miss this**. God used the following Scripture to change my entire life and my lifelong ministry forever. It is so very important for the Body of Christ to understand what God is saying to us through the prophet Isaiah.

Hear the Word of the Lord:

*Thus saith the Lord God: "Behold, I will lift up mine hand to the **Gentiles**, and set up my standard to the people: and they shall bring thy sons in **their** arms, and thy daughters shall be carried upon **their** shoulders"* (Isaiah 49:22 KJV, emphasis mine).

I believe this Scripture is so extremely important to our discussion of the *aliyah* that it merits the time and the words needed to dissect it so we can glean from it God's intended meaning. God is attempting to say something very important to the Body of Christ here, and we cannot *risk* missing it, nor do we *want* to miss it.

The passage opens with these words, *"Thus saith the Lord God."* The New International Version reads, *"This is what the Sovereign Lord says."* No matter which way we read it, the meaning is the same. What is being said is coming directly from God's lips to our ears. Anytime I read the words, "Thus saith the Lord" or "This is what the Sovereign Lord says," I sit up and take notice because it must be extremely important.

God goes on to say, *"Behold I will lift up mine hand unto the Gentiles."* In modern day English God is saying, "See I will **call** to the Gentiles." O.K., so who are these Gentiles God is referring to here? In God's economy of things a person is either a Jew or a Gentile. A Muslim is a Gentile, a Hindu is a Gentile, a Christian is a Gentile, a Buddhist is a Gentile, even an atheist is a Gentile. In other words, if a person is not a Jew he/she is a Gentile.

So, we now know that God is speaking to non-Jews in this verse so let's examine this idea a little closer. Which Gentiles in particular is He addressing? I believe the Gentiles He is referring to here are the Christians, the Body of Christ.

Can we possibly think for even a moment that Muslims would be involved in helping the Jews of the Diaspora return to the land of Israel? Now let me think about that one for a moment! *AH, I DON'T THINK SO!!* How about Hindus or Buddhists, or how about people of the Bahai Faith or perhaps the atheists? It is quite unlikely that any of the above would be willing to assist in this "Final Return" of the Jewish people. So then, simply by process of elimination we can come to the logical conclusion that God is speaking about the Body of Christ. Let's see what He says He wants to do with us concerning the *aliyah*.

God goes on to say:

"… and set up my standard to the people [the Gentiles, the Body of Christ] *and* **they** *shall bring thy sons in* **their** *arms, and thy daughters shall be carried on* **their** *shoulders."*

I firmly believe what we have just read is God saying to believers around the world that He is calling each of us—pastors, laypersons, missionaries, evangelists, church leaders, ministry leaders, cell group leaders and Sunday School teachers—to partner with Him in the return of His Chosen People to the land of their inheritance. As you are reading these words, this great exodus is taking place for the "sake of His Holy name" (Ezekiel 36:22) and for the redemption of all Israel (Romans 11:26), and He is calling each of us to help in this Holy work.

God, the Holy Spirit, took me directly to this Scripture in response to my tearful cry, *"God, who will help them?"* How much clearer could His answer have been? He wants us—the Body of Christ—to come alongside of Him to be His hands, to be His feet, and to be His heart in assisting His children in their return to the land of Israel from the nations. What an honor, what a privilege that the God of all creation would call upon Christians to be the ones to bring His children home.

I am reminded of a humbling experience that took place one afternoon while we were loading the ship with another load of precious Jewish cargo bound for the port of Haifa.

I had been assigned "step duty" by the leadership of the base for that day's sailing. "Step duty" was the most physically demanding duty that the volunteer team carried out on the day of sailing. It was my responsibility to stand at the bottom of the steps that ran up along the outside of the ship that the passengers used for their boarding process. We also used these same steps to hand-carry nearly seventeen tons of luggage onto the ship in preparation for sailing.

As the luggage dollies piled high with their cargo were brought to me and other waiting volunteers we would load the heavy bags onto our backs and climb the many steps to the deck level of the ship. There, just inside the main lobby area, another team of volunteers were waiting to carry the bags to the Repatriates' cabins where they would be eagerly awaiting their arrival.

It was on such a day that Linda wheeled a lovely Jewish lady who was confined to her wheelchair out to me as I stood at my post. This precious middle-aged woman was unable to stand, much less walk. We were quite accustomed to seeing this type of situation play out many times over and over again as God's prophetic Word was being fulfilled.

*"See, I will bring them from the land of the north and gather them from the ends of the earth. Among them will be the blind **and the lame**, expectant mothers and women in labor; a great throng will return"* Jeremiah 31:8, emphasis mine).

However; there was something unusual about this lovely Jewish lady. She was quite large and extremely heavy. I think a conservative guess of her weight was very close to three hundred pounds.

I immediately realized that I had to get her from the dock, up all of those many steep steps, and take her inside the main lobby of the ship. I took one look at her and then at the steps. I took a *second* look at her and then at the steps. I even did it a *third* time.

I am not a very large man, standing only five-feet-six-inches tall and weighing at that time around one hundred sixty pounds. How could I ever get this beautiful three-hundred-pound lady and her wheelchair up those steep shaky steps?

I did the only thing I knew to do. *I prayed*! I cried out to the *Enough God*, "Oh God, I can't do this in my own strength. I need Your help in my time of weakness. Please help me Lord God!"

I took the wheelchair by the two handles in the back while a young Ukrainian volunteer bent down, taking the small front wheels in his hands.

Picking up the lady in her wheelchair, we started up the steps with the Ukrainian volunteer going first in a backward position. We had only taken about two grueling steps when I suddenly realized that if we were going to be able to hold this lady level I would have to change my grip on the handles. As we paused for a few seconds I turned my hands upside down on the handles making it possible for me to lift the wheelchair higher, thus keeping our passenger as level as possible.

My volunteer friend and I took one tiring step at a time. Slowly, so very slowly, we were making our way up the steps with our precious cargo. It was when we reached somewhere near the half-way point of the steps that it suddenly happened!

I froze in my shoes! I could not take another step. Had God let me down? Had God somehow failed me after I had called upon Him for His help? Absolutely not! God was definitely still in control of this situation. The reason I froze where I stood isn't because I had lost the supernatural strength that God was giving me, but it was because of a startling revelation.

Just prior to freezing, I glanced over at my right hand holding onto the handle of the wheelchair, and the reality of this situation hit me squarely in my spirit. As I glanced at my hand I suddenly realized that the God of Abraham, Isaac and Jacob—the God of all creation, the God of the universe and, yes, the God of the Jews—had entrusted the well-being of one of His Chosen People into my feeble little hands.

I began to cry and even sob when this sobering fact hit my spirit. God trusted ME with one of His precious children! I could hardly believe it. Me—a middle-aged guy with Amish heritage from the farm lands of Central Pennsylvania. I shouted to the Lord from my spirit, "Why me Lord, why me? Apart from Christ, I am nothing. Why have you blessed me like this, allowing me to be a servant to your people?"

I realized that I could have dropped this lady perhaps killing her or crippling her even more so than she already was.

God's answer came swiftly when I heard His Spirit say, "I called you to this work because I knew you would leave everything to come."

I strongly believe that Barry Wagner was not God's first choice or even his best choice for the work I was doing then and for the work I am doing now. How many others had He called who simply did not respond before calling me for this work?

Does that make me someone special? Does that make me some kind of hero or someone to be admired? Absolutely not! I am simply a person who answered a new call on his life when it came. That is all I am and nothing more. I can assure you that every single individual working with Ezra International is just an "ordinary person, doing extraordinary things," with the help of God.

I am quite certain that there are far too many in the Body of Christ who do not accept the call on their lives because they feel inadequate. They feel they could never measure up to the task that God is calling them to. If you are one of these, please be reminded of this great truth: *God is not looking for ability. He is looking for availability.*

God is looking for men, women and young people who are willing to simply say, "Yes, Lord, here am I. Send me." That's it! It's that simple. That is exactly what God is looking for. Can you, or would you be willing to be counted in that number? The choice is yours. Once you say yes to God, you need only to hold on for the ride of your life and just let God be God, allowing the blessings from above to flow into you life.

Why Us, Lord?

"As a prisoner for the Lord, then, I urge you to live a life
worthy of the calling you have received."
Ephesians 4:1

When the reality of this call which God had placed upon all Christians had time to fully sink into my spirit, a very disturbing thought passed through my mind. Why would God place such an important call on the Body of Christ? How could He ever place the welfare of His Chosen People into the hands of each of us who profess Jesus Christ as Savior and Lord of our lives?

After the Holy Spirit revealed to me that it was we Gentiles who He wanted to labor with Him in the Jew's return to their own land, I screamed at God. I was laying on the floor in front of my desk in my study, and I yelled out in a very loud voice, *"Why us, Lord? Why us?"*

I didn't respond this way because I knew I would have to resign from our church and would have to give up my salary, the lovely parsonage, the paid utilities, the health insurance, and the wonderful people we had come to love. That had absolutely nothing to do with it. When you have a definite call on your life those material things really don't matter any longer, and their importance fades very quickly.

The reason I yelled out to God, "Why us, Lord," is because I have learned something about Jewish people over the years, and it is simply this: When a Jew hears the name Jesus or sees a cross or hears the word "Christian" he/she doesn't think of love and compassion, grace and kindness. In fact what they think of is far from it.

When most Jewish people hear the name Jesus or see a cross or hear the word "Christian" they think of the first crusades from 1096 to 1099. It was then that the crusaders came to Jerusalem from Western Europe to free the Holy Land from Muslim control.

The Jews of Jerusalem took refuge in the synagogues while the killing of Muslims was at its peak; however, the crusaders made little or no distinction between Muslims and Jews. The doors of the synagogues were chained shut before the fires were set. Jewish men, women, children and babies died a horrifying death while the crusaders rode around the burning building on their horses singing hymns to God, holding up their banners proudly displaying an insignia of the cross.

Secondly, the Jews think of the Spanish Inquisition which began in 1478, having been authorized by Pope Sixtus IV for King Ferdinand and Queen Isabella. It was during this period that Jews were forced to convert to Christianity or, many times, be put to death.

Once they gave into what was less than a sincere conversion they were subject to ecclesiastical discipline. During the years of the inquisition, if a Jew was found to be guilty of keeping any of their Jewish traditions, they were tried as heretics and burned alive.

Numbers vary as to how many Jews perished at the hands of the church during the Inquisition. Some records claim that the number was fewer than a few hundred while others claim the numbers exceeded well over two thousand and even higher. And it was all done under the "banner of the cross."

The sobering question we must ask ourselves is simply this: Were these horrors forced on humanity carried out by true Christian believers?

Here is a quote worth looking at:

"That religion, whose birthplace is Heaven and whose mission is love, should be propagated over the earth by means of racks and stakes, is utterly repugnant to all that we know of her and her Author. No; it was not Christianity, but its counterfeit, which the Inquisition was erected to promulgate. These were not priests, but demons; this was not a 'Holy Office,' but a DEN OF MURDERERS..." *

Thirdly, at the mention of the name Jesus, Jewish people also think of the Russian Pogroms which took place during the early part of the nineteen hundreds. It was during this time that over two thousand Jewish people of all ages were murdered, and their only crime was that they were Jews.

Reverend W.C. Stiles was in Russia during the pogroms of 1903. *"Under every kind of outrage they died, mostly at the door of their homes. They were babes, butchered at the breasts of their mothers. They were old men beaten down in the presence of their sons. They were delicate women violated and murdered in the sight of their own children."*

And then of course the worst event to ever take place in human history is what many Jewish people think of when they hear the name of Jesus or they see a cross. It is of course, the Holocaust.

Between 1939 and 1945, over six million Jews perished at the hands of a madman whose name was Adolph Hitler. This was a man who was steeped in "Replacement Theology." Here was a man who used the teachings of the German Lutheran church to justify the massacre of six million Jews.

After all if God has turned His back on the Jewish people, and if God has broken His covenant with them, and if God

---

* The Papacy: Its History, Dogmas, Genius, and Prospects, by Rev. J.A. Wylie, LL.D, Book III, Chapter 3

has rejected them for their unbelief, why then should they be important to us? That kind of crazed thinking is what I believe set the atmosphere for the Holocaust. That is why I refer to "Replacement Theology" as a theology from the pit of hell, a doctrine of demons.

Hitler's "Final Solution" was his plan to rid the entire world of the Jewish race. It failed! God will always have His covenant people, and He will always defend their land. The Jewish people continue to be the "Apple of His Eye." That hasn't changed.

It was this understanding about the Jewish people and how so many of them view the Christian faith that caused me to cry out to God, "God, why us?"

My heart was so terribly heavy as I pondered this calling placed on the Church by God Himself. How could God ever trust the well-being of any of His children to the Body of Christ—especially with our miserable history as it pertains to the treatment of Jewish people?

Michael Brown has written one of the most eye opening books on the subject of Jewish treatment by Christians that is available anywhere. It is entitled *Our Hands Are Stained With Blood*. This book has impacted my life as much as any book ever has, apart from the Bible. In his book Michael outlines the horrors that have been perpetrated on the Jewish people by so-called Christians throughout these many generations. This eye-opening book that should drive every believer to their knees in true repentance can be purchased on Amazon.com.

As I continued to cry out to God asking, "Why us Lord?" His answer came quickly. I heard the voice of the Holy Spirit deep within my spirit say, *"Barry, for centuries the Church has been a curse to my people, but now I want the Church to be a **blessing** to them. I want to give the Church a second chance."*

Wherever I share this message I tell people, "Thank God we serve a God of second chances!" If God was not a God of second chances, not one of us would be where he is today.

Pastor, you would not be serving that church you are presently serving. Sir, you would not be sitting in that pew on Sunday morning. Madam, your name would not be written in the Lamb's Book of Life. Teenager, you would not be where you are in Christ today if God was not a God of second chances.

Church, God is so gracious and so full of mercy toward us that He is giving us a second chance to do it right this time as we become servants to the Jewish people. Please, let's not miss this wonderful opportunity He is blessing us with. Let's hear what He is saying concerning the return of the millions of Jews from the nations of the world to their "Promised Land."

Let's all be willing to give of our time, our prayers and our resources to partner with God and allow ourselves to be used by Him in the gathering of His people, fulfilling Bible prophecy in the process.

I have felt very strongly for many years that this thing God has called us to do among the Jewish people, we are not worthy to do. We do not deserve the honor of the task that He has bestowed upon us; and yet He has done just that.

The apostle Paul wrote in Ephesians 3:1:

"For this reason I, Paul, the prisoner of Christ Jesus for the sake of you Gentiles ... "

Just as Paul declared that he was a prisoner of Christ, I feel that I am a prisoner of the *aliyah* as do many thousands of other Christians around the world. They have heard the clarion call of God to the Body of Christ, and they, too, have picked up the mantle and are now assisting in the prophetic "Final Return" of the Jewish people. They are doing it through their prayers, by giving of their financial resources, and even by going into the nations as volunteers to stand with God's people in their time of destiny.

A dear friend asked me this sobering question several years ago. He asked, "Barry, I know how much you loved being a pastor, the passion you have for preaching, how much you loved your people, and now you are doing the work of *aliyah*. Could you ever see yourself being a pastor again?"

I was somewhat startled by my quick response to my friend's question when I said, "As long as there is one Jewish person left in the former Soviet Union, I cannot do anything other than what I am doing." I am truly a prisoner of the *aliyah*.

My dear friend, this calling is not placed upon a chosen few. God has called the Body of Christ—the Church—to become the instrument in His hands to carry "their sons in *our* arms and to carry their daughters on *our* shoulders." Are you willing to say, "Yes, Lord, here am I; use me?" Or will you say, "I really don't want to be involved in God's plan for the Jewish people and the land of Israel?" Of course the choice is yours. Nobody can make that decision for you.

I can tell you this without any reservation whatsoever. The *aliyah* is the closest thing to the heart of God at this moment in human history. As for me, I just want to be laboring at the task that is closest to Abba's heart.

At the close of this book I will explain how you can become prayerfully and financially involved in assisting God's children to return to the land of their inheritance through the ministry of Ezra International. You no longer need to simply sit idly by, watching Bible prophecy being fulfilled. You can be a part of it, and your life will be richly blessed because of your decision.

"I will bless those who bless you and whoever curses you I will curse; and all peoples on earth will be blessed through you" (Genesis 12:3).

Chapter Seventeen

"Jews–Rejected By God?"

"I ask then: Did God reject His people? By no means!
God did not reject his people, whom He foreknew."
Romans 11:1a, 2a

In previous chapters we have lightly touched on the erroneous teachings of "Replacement Theology," which teaches that God has rejected the Jewish people. This theology also teaches that He has forsaken them, He has turned His face from them, and He has broken His covenant with them.

Does this teaching have a valid claim? Is it accurate? Does it have merit? Can it be supported by Scripture? I have no intention of writing a long discourse on this subject for there are much more qualified people of the Christian faith than I who can do a far better job of discrediting such false teaching. I will leave that task to them.

I do, however, wish to share just a few of the many Scriptures of the Old Testament (the *Tanakh*) and the New Testament that makes it abundantly clear that God has not, nor will He *ever*, forsake or reject the Jewish people.

We can begin with the Scripture we looked at earlier taken from the book of Genesis 13:15. God made an unconditional covenant with Abram and the Israelites when He declared:

"All the land that you see I will give to you and your offspring **forever.***"* (emphasis mine)

When God says *forever*, I really do believe that He means *forever*.

How about Genesis 17:7, 8?

"I will establish my covenant as an **everlasting** *covenant between me and you and your descendants after you for the generations to come, to be your God and the God of your descendants after you. The whole land of Canaan, where you are now an alien, I will give as an* **everlasting** *possession to you and your descendants after you; and I will be their God"* (emphasis mine).

Once again, I truly believe that when God says an everlasting covenant He means everlasting.

Wow, take a close look at what God says through the prophet Jeremiah about the Israelites and Israel:

This is what the Lord says, "He who appoints the sun to shine by day, who decrees the moon and stars to shine by night, who stirs up the sea so that its waves roar-the Lord Almighty is His name; Only if these decrees vanish from my sight," declares the Lord, "will the descendants of Israel ever cease to be a nation before me" (Jeremiah 31:35,36).

God continues:

"Only if the heavens above can be measured and the foundations of the earth below be searched out will I reject all the descendants of Israel because of all they have done," declares the Lord (Jeremiah 31:37).

It simply amazes me how anyone can read the above scripture and still believe that God has rejected His chosen people, the Jews!

God makes it so crystal clear that He will reject the descendants of Israel ONLY when the heavens can be measured and the foundations of the earth be searched out— both of which we know can never happen.

God speaks of the Israelites—not the Church—this way in Ezekiel 20:41,42:

"I will accept you as fragrant incense when I bring you out from the nations and gather you from the countries where you have been scattered, and I will show myself holy among you in the sight of the nations. Then you will know that I am the Lord, when I bring you into the land of Israel, the land I had sworn with uplifted hand to give to your fathers."

That doesn't sound to me that God has forgotten or forsaken the Jewish people. It sounds to me that they have a very bright future ahead of them as God's eternal plan continues to unfold—as He is gathering them to the land of Israel in the *aliyah*.

God continues speaking of His love for Israel and the Jewish people in Ezekiel's prophecy:

This is what the Sovereign Lord says; "When I gather the people of Israel from the nations where they have been scattered, I will show myself holy among them in the sight of the nations. Then they will live in their own land, which I gave to my servant Jacob. They will live there in safety and will build houses and plant vineyards; they will live in safety when I inflict punishment on all their neighbors who maligned them. Then they will know that I am the Lord their God" (Ezekiel 28:25,26).

Do we need any more proof that God has a special plan for His chosen people and the land of Israel? If we do, let's take a quick look at Ezekiel 39:25–29:

Therefore this is what the Sovereign Lord says: "I will now bring Jacob (Israel) back from captivity and will have compassion on all the people of Israel, and I will be zealous for my holy name. They will forget their shame and all the unfaithfulness they showed toward me when they lived in safety in their land with no one to make them afraid. When I have brought them back from the nations and have gathered them from the countries of their enemies, I will show myself holy through them in the sight of many nations. Then they will know that I am the Lord their God, for though I sent them into exile among the nations, [70 AD, the Diaspora] I will gather them to their own land, (Israel) not leaving any behind. I will no longer hide my face from them, for I will pour out my Spirit [Holy Spirit] on the house of Israel," declares the Sovereign Lord (emphasis mine).

We must keep in mind that the Scriptures we have been looking at are prophetic Scriptures, speaking of things to come. Now if God has forsaken and rejected the Jewish people these Scriptures would have no serious meaning whatsoever. But God said through the prophets that He would one day do all of these things and so much more as it pertains to the Jewish people, and you can rest assured that if God said He will do something, He will do it!

How about one more confirmation from Scripture that God has kept His covenant with Israel? Look at what King David wrote in the Psalms.

*"He remembers His covenant **forever**, the word He commanded, for a thousand generations, the covenant He made with Abraham, the oath He swore to Isaac. He confirmed it to Jacob as a decree, to Israel as an **everlasting** covenant: 'To you I will give the land of Canaan as the portion you will inherit'"* (Psalm 105:8-11).

I can just hear our skeptic friends saying to themselves right now, "All of these Scriptures are taken from the Old Testament. Show me proof in the New Testament that God still loves the Jewish people and He continues to have His hand upon them?"

Well, my dear skeptic friends, we could fill many more pages from the prophetic word of God that declares His unconditional love for Israel and His people and His eternal plans for them, but time and space do not allow such an in-depth study of the subject. So now, let's take a look into the New Testament shall we? The apostle Paul made it perfectly clear that God has NOT rejected the Jewish people.

Let's see what Paul has to tell us.

"I ask then: Did God reject His people, (the Jews)? By no means! I am an Israelite myself, a descendant of Abraham, from the tribe of Benjamin. God DID NOT reject His people, whom He foreknew" (Romans 11:1,2a, emphasis mine).

How much plainer does it have to be? Either we believe the Word of God, or we don't. I choose to believe the words of Paul when he says, "God *did not* reject his people.

How about this verse? How does our skeptic friend who continues to hold onto the false teachings of "Replacement Theology" explain this one away?

Again I ask: "Did they [the Jews] *stumble so as to fall beyond recovery? Not at all! Rather, because of their transgression, salvation has come to the Gentiles to make Israel envious. But if their transgression means riches for the world, and their loss means riches for the Gentiles, how much greater riches will their fullness bring?"* Romans 11:11, 12, emphasis mine).

The apostle Paul continues in Romans 11:25 through 27. *"I do not want you to be ignorant of this mystery, brothers, so that you may not be conceited: Israel has experienced a hardening in part until the full number of the Gentiles has come in. And so ALL Israel will be saved, as it is written: the Deliverer will come from Zion; He will turn godlessness away from Jacob (Israel). And this is my covenant with them when I take away their sins'"* (emphasis mine).

Again, if God is not going to do these things then why did Paul ever write of them? He makes it very clear that these are things that are to come at the end of the age. It is also very clear that God has not forsaken His chosen people, nor will He ever do so.

Let's take a look at Matthew's gospel to see what Jesus himself had to say about the love God has for the Jewish people.

"O Jerusalem, Jerusalem, [Jews] *you who kill the prophets and stone those sent to you, how often I have longed to gather your children together, as a hen gathers her chicks under her*

wings, but you were not willing. Look, your house is left to you desolate. For I tell you, you (the Jewish people) will not see me again until you say, 'Blessed is He who comes in the name of the Lord'" (Matthew 23:37-39, emphasis mine).

Have you ever considered the fact that the return of our Lord Jesus Christ is hinged to the Jewish people? Jesus said, *"You will not see me again until you* [the Jewish people] *say, 'Blessed is He who comes in the name of the Lord.'"*

Now if that is what Jesus is waiting for before He returns, it certainly sounds to me like God has a very definite plan for the Jewish people, the land of Israel, as well as for you and for me.

It is impossible to separate your future, the future of all the nations, and the future of all mankind from the future of the Jewish people and the land of Israel. Keep your eyes on Israel. She is God's eternal time clock for world events.

Chapter Eighteen

Time Is Running Out

"What you are about to do, do quickly."
Jesus of Nazareth

The greatest enemy of the Jewish people of the former Soviet Union countries is not anti-Semitism—as horrible as that is. It is not even the terrible economy which has reduced these people to a second class—and many times even to a third class—life style, stripping them of any self-worth and dignity. The greatest enemy of God's chosen people is *time*. Time is quickly running out for many of the Jews of the FSU countries where Ezra International is laboring.

In 1991, when the walls of Communism fell across the former Soviet Union, the doors for legal immigration of the Jews were thrown wide open. Since that historic event took place, over one-and-a-half million Jewish people of those countries have fled to Israel.

The greatest concern we have is that those same doors that were so quickly thrown open will soon be slammed shut just as quickly.

Today we are seeing so many sweeping and dangerous changes taking place in Russia. President Putin is putting severe pressure on Ukraine and Georgia as well as other countries to come back under Russia's control. He is using oil exports and high oil prices to pressure these independent countries to fall in line and once again march to his orders.

This former KGB leader has now taken away freedom of the press and freedom of the airways in his country. Personal and religious liberties are beginning to fall by the wayside. He is working hand-in-hand with today's Hitler— Mahmoud Ahmadinejad, the President of Iran—to aid him in the completion of Iran's nuclear capabilities, which is a serious threat to Israel and the rest of the free world.

President Putin recently made a state visit to Iran to shore up his relationship with Ahmadinejad. This is the man who is calling for Israel to be wiped off the map, and he declares to the world that the Holocaust never took place. This was the first visit by a Russian president to Iran since World War I.

Russian population is now in a very serious decline and getting worse with each passing year. At present there are only 10.7 births for every 15 deaths. Those figures translate into an annual population decline of between 750,000 and 800,000 persons per year.

A second reason for a decline in population is the abortion issue. In 2004 there were 1.6 million abortions and only 1.5 million births.

A third serious problem that Russia is facing is the vast number of people leaving Russia, seeking a better life for their families in other countries. In 1970, for an example, Russia had the third largest Jewish population (2,150,000) in the world preceded only by the United States and Israel. By 2005 the Jewish population fell to 235,000, in mainland Russia due to vast numbers making their *aliyah* to Israel. This does not include the other countries of the former Soviet Union where there is still an estimated one-and-a-half million Jews remaining.

The handwriting is on the wall. Russia cannot allow their population numbers to continue to fall at such an alarming rate. The quickest way to stop such a decline is to close the doors of legal immigration out of the country once again. It is not a matter of *if* the doors close on our Jewish brothers and sisters, it is a matter of *when*.

There is a saying in Ukraine that was shared with me by an elderly Jewish man. It says, "As the winds blow in Russia, it's not long until the same winds blow in Ukraine."

Every person who is now assisting in the *aliyah* or who has been a part of it in the past shares the same concerns. We all feel keenly that the closing of the doors for Jews to leave the former Soviet Union countries will begin in Russia and then spread to many, if not all, of the FSU countries.

I have had such a sense of anxiety in my spirit for nearly ten years now due to this reality, and it only grows more intense with each passing month. Therefore, what we must do, we must do quickly. When those doors of immigration close the lives of the Jewish population will be hanging in the balance.

At the close of the movie "Schindler's List" we see Oscar Schindler preparing to go into exile after having been declared to be an enemy of Germany. The scene is outside the factory where he employed over twelve-hundred Jewish men and women whose freedom he had purchased with his own financial resources. He spent everything he had in order to save the lives of these Jewish people.

To pay tribute to this Righteous Gentile, a Rabbi that he had saved had fashioned a gold ring from the gold filling of one of the Jewish workers. As the Rabbi handed the ring to Schindler it was accidentally dropped and fell to the ground. Both men bent down to pick it up at the same time. It was then that Oscar Schindler began to cry saying to the Rabbi, "I could have saved more." The Rabbi answered, "No, you did everything you could have done." He said, "In the Jewish tradition it is said that if a person saves one life he saves the world."

Schindler then pointed to his gold lapel pin and said, "Why did I keep this? If I had only sold it I could have saved one more." And then he pointed to his car and once again said, "The car—why didn't I sell the car? I could have saved ten more." Because of Oscar Schindler's compassion and his willingness to spend his last cent, he has been credited for saving over one thousand, two hundred Jewish lives. He is now counted as one of the Righteous Gentiles by the Jewish people.

I have visited Oscar Schindler's grave on Mount Zion in Jerusalem on several occasions. As I place a stone on his grave in the Jewish tradition, I cannot help but feel somewhat of a connection with this man because of his love for God's people and his willingness to do whatever was necessary to save as many of their lives as possible.

Every time I helped a Jewish person down the steps of the ship and placed their feet on Israeli soil for the first time I would say under my breath, "One more Lord, one more of your children safely at home in their Promised Land." "Thank you Lord."

Every time I receive the monthly reports from the various countries we are working in, listing the names of the Jewish people we assisted that month in their return to Israel, I can't help but say, "Eighty-three more Lord," or, "Sixty-two more Lord," or whatever the numbers may be. That is what the *aliyah* is all about, helping God's children return to the land of their inheritance. It is only in Israel that they will be able to experience their God-appointed destiny.

Time for the Jewish people of the former Soviet Union countries is quickly running out. The doors can slam shut any day now leaving them stranded once again. My dear friends, we cannot, we *must* not allow one precious Jewish soul be left behind. Not on our watch!

God says through the prophet Ezekiel:

"Then they will know that I am the Lord their God, for though I sent them into exile among the nations, I will gather

*them to their own land, **not leaving any behind*** (Ezekiel 39:28, emphasis mine).

"Not leaving any behind." That is Abba's heart, and that is the heart of Ezra International. It is that deep commitment that keeps the entire Ezra team pushing forward even when a situation looks to be impossible in the flesh. We all know that no matter how badly we want to see the Jewish people home in Israel, God wants them to be home even more.

You see, God knows where everyone of His children are, even if Ezra International doesn't. God will go to any lengths to reach them in regards to their return to the land of Israel.

My phone rang at the Ezra office one afternoon in 2001, and Mel Hoelzle was on the other end. He said, "Barry, I need you and Viktor to go into Azerbaijan to begin a new work there. We know that there are over 35,000 Jewish people there who we must help."

My response to Mel was, "I will make arrangements to go immediately." Actually, I was too embarrassed to tell him that I had no idea where Azerbaijan was located, so I had to go to the internet and pull up a world map to learn of my future destination. Mel knows that I am willing to go anywhere in the world at any time to locate and assist the Jewish people in their return.

After connecting with Viktor Mykhailov—our number one man in the Kiev office—we made arrangements to fly from Kiev to Baku, the capital city of Azerbaijan.

As I just said, God is willing to go to any lengths to insure that His people receive the help they so desperately need. Here I was in Kiev with no visa for Azerbaijan. Viktor and I went to the Azerbaijan Embassy for me to apply for a visa. We knew that flights from Kiev to Baku only flew on Tuesdays and Fridays, so we had very little time for the visa process.

We made our first visit to the embassy on Monday morning with all the necessary documents and letters of invitation, etc. I was told to return the morning of the next day to pick up my visa. This would still leave us enough time to catch the Tuesday flight to Baku. Upon my arrival at the embassy I was informed that there was a problem, and I would not be able to receive my visa until Thursday morning.

As instructed, we returned to the embassy on Thursday morning around 9:00 A.M. only to be told, once again, that there was a problem and the visa would not be ready until 4:30 P.M. Now things began to become quite serious. We had booked flights for early the next day, and we knew that the embassy was not open on Fridays. So if I did not receive my visa by no later than 5:00 P.M. that day I would not be able to fly to Azerbaijan due to my tight schedule for my return to the U.S. I would simply be out of days, since the next flight to Baku was not until the following Tuesday.

We arrived at the embassy around 4:15 P.M. As we were called to the gentlemen's office who had the final say as to who receives visas and who doesn't, we were shocked to once again hear him say that there was a problem with my request.

Throughout that day we had the entire Ezra staff praying for this much-needed visa. To save precious time in this last face-to-face interview with the embassy official I just had Viktor do all the talking so he would not have to translate for me. As Viktor talked, I prayed. At times I remember feeling very uncomfortable in my spirit. I could tell that the conversation was not going well in my favor.

At what seemed to be the most critical point, I finally did what I should have done three days earlier, I turned the entire situation over to God. I said, "God, you were able to part the Red Sea for the Israelites, and I know if it is your will you can part the red tape that we are facing."

I knew that if the visa was not granted by 5:00 P.M. there would be no hope of my making this critical journey. Remember what I said in an earlier chapter? I said, "God is never late," and once again He proved it to me. At exactly 4:59 P.M. I heard the sound of the visa stamp as the embassy person in charge stamped the visa into my passport. Just one minute before the drop dead deadline. Like I said, "God is never late, *but* He is never early either."

Upon our arrival at the Baku airport we were met by a pastor who had been pastoring an underground church in the city for a number of years prior to the fall of Communism. After our initial greetings he said, "Barry, there is a group of Jewish people living in the mountains in the northern part of this country. I think it is very important that you make contact with them to make them aware of the help Ezra International can give them to make their *aliyah*."

Early the next morning the pastor assisted Viktor and me in hiring a car and a driver who would be willing to drive us the five hours into the mountains of Azerbaijan over the horribly rough roads.

I must tell you, that ride was one of the longest rides of my entire life. For five hours our driver weaved and dodged the huge potholes in roads that had not been repaired in many years. I have a real problem with motion sickness, and this ride was worse than any time I had ever spent on fishing boats in the rough waters of the Gulf of Mexico or on cruise ships in the Atlantic Ocean or the Caribbean Sea.

Upon our arrival in the small village of Quba we were directed to the Jewish synagogue where we had the honor and privilege of meeting the local rabbi. At first he seemed somewhat suspicious of our motive for being there. After sharing the unconditional love for the Jewish people that God had placed into our hearts and how we would like to assist anyone from his village to make their *aliyah*, he soon warmed up to us. It wasn't long before we were laughing together and sometimes crying together.

After hearing of the terrible poverty that he and his people were living in, it was soon decided that Ezra would start a monthly feeding program for the people of his synagogue.

During my second visit to this village and the synagogue, the rabbi told me something quite interesting. He said, "Barry, our people have had a presence here in this village for over two thousand years." I was shocked when the reality of what he told me fully hit my spirit. This rabbi just told me that his people have been in this village since the Diaspora—the dispersion of the Jews of Israel after the destruction of the Holy Temple and the city of Jerusalem by the Roman Empire.

For over two thousand years they have been settled here in this quant little village of Quba, Azerbaijan, but now for some untold reason many of them want to immigrate to Israel. Praise God for His faithfulness to his people. But what could it be that is drawing these Mountain Jews to the land of Israel after being firmly planted in Quba for over two thousand years? Can it be the Holy Spirit of God? Of course it is. After all, He said He would call them from out of every nation. From the four corners of the earth He would call them. Now, the Jews of Quba, Azerbaijan, have heard His call, and with the help of Ezra International they are going home.

I would like to encourage you to stop your reading at this point, go to your computer and Google "Mountain Jews." The next thing you see on your screen will be the history of these fascinating Jews from the mountains of northern Azerbaijan.

No matter where God's children are found—in the mountains of Azerbaijan or the waste lands of Siberia, on the sixteenth floor of an apartment building in a major city or in a two room shack with dirt floors, in a farming village or sleeping next to a boiler in the basement of a commercial building—our calling remains the same. We are to stand with our Jewish brothers and sisters and to love them with an unconditional love.

Jesus said, *"As you have done it to the least of these my brethren, you have done it unto me"* (Matthew 25:40).

It is always that unconditional love that touches the heart of every living soul.

I had the privilege to take part in an Ezra-sponsored reception recently in Kiev, Ukraine. Our special guests included the Israeli consul, the undersecretary to the Israeli Ambassador, and other guests from Israel along with Sergi Popov, a world renowned violinist who is also a dear personal friend.

At one point the Israeli consul asked me, "Barry, why are you and Ezra International working so hard to help our people make their *aliyah* to Israel?" I simply responded, "because the God of the Jews—your God, the God of Abraham, Isaac and Jacob, the same God we serve—has called us to this Holy work. We must do it, and we must continue doing it until the last Jew is at home in Israel from the FSU countries."

I saw tears begin to well up in his eyes. The undersecretary to the Israeli Ambassador was struggling to hold back tears as well. What was it that these two men were responding to? Perhaps, in part, it was the words that I spoke, but even more powerful than the words was the unconditional love of Christ they were experiencing from a Gentile. The Bible tells us that *"Love never fails"* (I Corinthians 13:8a).

I had a wonderful opportunity not only to share God's love for them and my love for them but *your* love as well. I told my new Jewish friends that, "I know it seems like the entire world is against you, and unfortunately most of it is, but I want you to know something today: you are not alone. There are several million evangelical Christians from around the world who love you and who pray for you. These same Christians give of their time and their financial resources to help your people make their *aliyah*. We do it because God loves you and your people so much that He has called us to stand alongside of your people in their *aliyah* so that none will be left behind."

So my dear friends, please be reminded that time is quickly running out for the Jews of the former Soviet Union countries, and what we must do, we must do quickly. On behalf of the more than one million Jews still remaining in those countries may I ask you to become involved in this "Final Return" of the Jewish people to the land of Israel? There is so little precious time remaining for them to be able to leave, and they cannot do it without our help.

Chapter Nineteen

Anti-Semitism Is Sweeping the Globe

*"The only thing we learn from history is that
we learn nothing from history."*
Friedrich Hegal

After the hellish days of the Spanish Inquisition, the Crusades, the Russian pogroms and the horrors of the Holocaust, it would seem logical to me that mankind would have learned at least a little something from these terrible events. But did it? Did we learn anything at all?

Did we learn the truth about the effects of hate crimes, and the untold misery they bring upon millions of innocent people around the world as they are carried out? More often than not it is the children and the elderly who pay the greatest price for man's hatred of people of other nations, or people of a different color, people from a different society or people of a different religion.

After sixty years of living, I have come to the frightening conclusion that "the only thing we learn from history is that we learn nothing from history." The realities of that conclusion can have devastating effects on every human being on the face of the planet. It is truly that serious.

Here we are, living in the year 2007, and yet we are witnessing many of the same horrible events that lead up to the Holocaust.

Many times when I am addressing a congregation I will say to them, "I am so thankful that we have grown as a world community beyond the days of the Holocaust, and we will never see anything like that in the future again—aren't you?" Many times I will hear several people from the crowd shout, "Amen!"

It is then that I break the news to them that it can happen again. Even now we are seeing the same pattern unfold around the world concerning the hatred of the Jewish people.

The fires of anti-Semitism are sweeping across Europe today as it did just prior to the dreadful Holocaust years. Here is just a very small sampling of what is taking place all across Europe.

In Britian: The cover of the *New Statesman*, a left-wing magazine depicted a large Star of David stabbing the Union Jack. Oxford professor Tom Paulin, a noted poet, told an Egyptian interviewer that American Jews who move to the West Bank and Gaza "should be shot dead." A Jewish *yeshiva* student reading the Psalms was stabbed 27 times on a London bus.

"Anti-Semitism," wrote a columnist in the Spectator, "has become respectable at London dinner tables." She quoted one member of the House of Lords. "The Jews have been asking for it, and now, thank God, we can say what we think at last."

In Italy: The daily paper *La Stampa* published a cartoon on the front page: A tank emblazoned with the Jewish star points its gun at the baby Jesus, who pleads, "Surely they don't want to kill me again?"

In Germany: A rabbinical student was beaten up in downtown Berlin, and a grenade was thrown into a Jewish cemetery. Thousands of neo-Nazis held a rally and marched near a synagogue on the Jewish Sabbath. Graffiti appeared on a synagogue in the western town of Herford: "Six million were not enough."

In Ukraine: Skinheads attacked Jewish worshippers and smashed the windows of Kiev's main synagogue.

Here is just one of many personal examples I could share with you concerning how the tide of anger and hatred of the Jewish people is so common in Ukraine.

After the wonderful moving concert with Sergi Popov that I mentioned earlier we were quite surprised by the scene that had developed just outside the concert hall.

As we peered through the windows and the glass doors we could see hundreds of policemen in full riot gear lining the sidewalk and the streets in all directions. We could also see several hundred members of the Nationalist Party— skinheads who are part of this neo-Nazi hate group which is calling for the extermination of the Jewish people.

I have on film a member of this same organization during an anti-Semitic march through Red Square in Moscow with over ten thousand people participating, shouting into the camera, "The problems in Russia could all be solved if every Russian would just kill one Jew."

As I stepped out of the concert hall I could feel the extremely heavy tension in the air. I remember one of our security people placing his hand in the middle of my back and whispering in my ear, "Barry, don't say a word, just keep walking." It was necessary for us to walk several blocks through this crowd of anti-Semitic fanatics to reach the restaurant where the reception was being held for the Israeli dignitaries.

I have always worn a beautiful blue and white Star of David on the lapel of my suit jacket whenever and wherever I speak. I want the world to know of my personal stand and commitment to the Jewish people, and it is my way of identifying with them.

So here I am, being escorted through this crowd of hate mongers with a Star of David in plain view for all to see. My interpreter, Anna Nikitenko, who was also being escorted by the same security person noticed my Star of David and said, "Barry, take that off your jacket." When I failed to respond she said it again.

My response to her was, "Anna, there is no way I will remove this Star of David from my jacket. I will never allow hate filled people to compromise my stand with Israel. If we can't stand with our Jewish friends during the hard times, we have no business standing with them during the easy times."

In Holland: An anti-Israel demonstration featured swastikas, photos of Hitler, and chants of "Sieg Heil" and "Jews into the sea."

In Slovakia: The Jewish cemetery of Kosice was invaded and 135 tombstones destroyed. But nowhere have the flames of anti-Semitism burned more furiously than in France.

In France: According to police, metropolitan Paris has seen 10 to 12 anti-Jewish incidents per day since Easter of 2001.

Walls in Jewish neighborhoods have been defaced with slogans proclaiming "Jews to the gas chambers" and "Death to the Jews." The weekly journal *Le Nouvel Observateur* published an appalling libel: It said Israeli soldiers rape Palestinian women, so that their relatives will kill them to preserve "family honor."

"At the start of the 21st century," writes Pierre-Andre Tagueff, a well-known social scientist, in a new book, "We are discovering that Jews are once again select targets of violence ... hatred of the Jews has returned to France." But of course, it never left. Not France. Not Europe!

They are making a grievous mistake. For if today the violence and vitriol are aimed at the Jews, tomorrow they will be aimed at the Christians. A timeless lesson of history is that it rarely ends with the Jews. The Nazis first set out to incinerate the Jews, but in the end, all of Europe was ablaze.

Information by: *Jeff Jacoby of The Boston Globe as it appeared in Prophecy in the News.*

Here is a short news article from UCSJ News, dated October 5, 2004.

Rabbi Beaten in Kiev, Jews Threatened in Donetsk

More anti-Semitic incidents were reported over the last week in Ukraine, where the number of violent acts against Jews has sharply increased in recent months. On September 28, 2004, the Russian Jewish web site www.Jewish.ru reported that Rabbi Moshe Tyler, a Chabad Lubavitch rabbi working in Ukraine, was beaten on a downtown Kiev street while walking with his wife. A group of unidentified people ran up to the rabbi and hit him several times in the face before running off. Rabbi Tyler reported the attack to police.

Meanwhile in Donetsk, where a Yeshiva student was assaulted in August, the situation for Jews seems to be sharply deteriorating. Members of the Jewish community told Jewish.ru that, "Over the past six months there has been ten times the number of anti-Semitic acts as there have been in the past ten years." On October 4, 2004, Jewish.ru reported that several incidents of anti-Semitic harassment took place over the just concluded Jewish holiday of Sukkot. The most prominent of these incidents happened in the center of town, when a group of men shadowed a religious procession near a synagogue and threatened to kill Jews. One of the anti-Semites reportedly vowed: "We will hang all of you who weren't killed in Dachau."

You may be somewhat surprised about what you have just read about anti-Semitism across Europe, but what about America? Surely in America—that is so "tolerant" of everybody and everything unless, of course, it pertains to Christianity—we would never see anything remotely connected to anti-Semitism, would we? Let's examine Lisa J. Huriash's story written for the South Florida Sun-Sentinel:

Anti-Semitic Crimes Rise in Florida

The number of anti-Semitic hate crimes in Florida increased again last year, according to a study released Monday by the Jewish Anti-Defamation League.

The annual ADL Audit of Anti-Semitic Incidents reported 173 incidents in the state in 2004. That's up from 102 in 2003 and 93 in 2002.

"It's troubling because that's a dramatic and graphic reminder of the resilience of bigotry," said Arthur Teitelbaum, ADL's Southern Area director. "Hatred is learned. It can be an aggressive cancer in society, and it needs to be opposed at every level."

In 2004, Florida Jews were the victims of 144 incidents of harassment and 29 incidents of vandalism. A middle-school student in Boca Raton found a swastika and the words "Die, Jews, Die" written in a textbook. A child was sent to an elementary school's Halloween parade in Miami Beach dressed as Adolf Hitler. A Jewish student at a middle school in North Miami was bullied at school through physical assault and taunted with Holocaust references to pizza ovens. The windows of a Jewish day school in North Miami were covered with feces. A synagogue in West Palm Beach was defaced with a swastika, and a front lawn in Key West had an anti-Semitic message placed on a cross.

Teitelbaum said anti-Semitism is on the rise in countries such as France, Germany and Britain, and although Florida is not close to that violent atmosphere, it is "still deeply disturbing that anti-Semitism remains a problem in America."

Rabbi Solomon Schiff, executive vice president of the Rabbinical Association of Greater Miami said he found the new statistics upsetting.

"It's very disturbing in the light of so much knowledge the world has had with anti-Semitism and the results of it, like the Holocaust, that this should still be going on," he said.

Rabbi Alan Sherman, executive vice president of the Palm Beach County Board of Rabbis in West Palm Beach, said the numbers are "still quite manageable" and might reflect a rise in the state's population.

The number of reported incidents rose nationally as well. In 2004, there were 1,821 anti-Semitic incidents, an increase over the 1,557 in 2003 and 1,559 in 2002. The states with the highest total incidents were New York with 350, New Jersey with 297, and California with 237, followed by Florida.

Below is an account of an anti-Semitic riot on the campus of San Francisco State University in May of 2002. This account was written by Lauri Zoloth, the director of the Jewish Studies program at SFSU.

Dear Colleagues,

Today, all day, I have been listening to the reactions of students, parents, and community members who were on campus yesterday. I have received emails and phone calls from around the country, worried for both my personal safety on the campus and for the entire intellectual project of having a Jewish Studies program and recruiting students to a campus that in the last month has become a venue for hate speech and anti-Semitism. After nearly seven years as director of Jewish Studies, and after nearly two decades of life here as a student, faculty member, and wife of the Hillel rabbi, after years of patient work and difficult civic discourse, I am saddened to see SFSU return to its notoriety as a place that teaches anti-Semitism, hatred for America, and above all else, hatred for the Jewish State of Israel—a state that I cherish. I cannot fully express what it feels like to have to walk across campus daily, past maps of the Middle East that do not include Israel; past posters of cans of soup with labels on them of drops of blood and dead babies, labeled "canned Palestinian children meat, slaughtered according to Jewish rites under American license"; past poster after poster calling out "Zionism=racism, and Jews=Nazis." This is not civic discourse, this is not free speech, and this is not the Weimar Republic with brown shirts it cannot control. This is the casual introduction of the medieval blood libel and virulent hatred smeared around our campus in a manner so ordinary that it hardly excites concern—except if you are a Jew and you understand that hateful words have always led to hateful deeds.

Yesterday, the hatred coalesced in a hate mob. Yesterday's Peace In The Middle East Rally was completely organized by the Hillel students—mostly 18 and 19 years old. They spoke about their lives at SFSU and of their support for Israel, and they sang of peace. They wore new Hillel t-shirts that said "Peace" in English, Hebrew and Arabic. A Russian immigrant, in his new English, spoke of loving his new country, a haven from anti-Semitism. A sophomore spoke about being here only one year and about the support and community she found at the Hillel House. Both spoke of how hard it was to live as a Jew on this campus, how isolating, how terrifying. A surfer guy spoke of his love of Jesus and his support for Israel, and a young freshman earnestly asked for a moment of silence, and all the Jews stood still listening as the shouted hate of the counter-demonstrators filled the air with abuse.

As soon as the community supporters left, the 50 students who remained praying their traditional afternoon prayers or chatting or cleaning up after the rally and talking were surrounded by a large, angry crowd of Palestinians and their supporters. But they were not calling for peace. They screamed at us to "go back to Russia," and they screamed that they would kill us all, and other terrible things. They surrounded the praying students and the older women who are our elder college participants, who survived the Shoah, who helped shape the Bay Area peace movement, only to watch as a threatening crowd shoved the Hillel students against the wall of the plaza. I had invited members of my

Orthodox community to join us, members of my Board of Visitors, and we stood there in despair. Let me remind you that building the SFSU Jewish Studies program, we asked the same people for their support and that our Jewish community—who pays for the program once as taxpayers and again as Jews—generously support our program. Let me remind you that ours is arguably one of the Jewish Studies programs in the country most devoted to peace, justice and diversity since our inception.

As the counter-demonstrators poured into the plaza screaming at the Jews to "Get out or we will kill you" and "Hitler did not finish the job," I turned to the police and to every administrator I could find and asked them to remove the counter-demonstrators from the Plaza, to maintain the separation of 100 feet that we had been promised. The police told me that they had been told not to arrest anyone and that if they did, "It would start a riot." Finally, Fred Astren the Northern California Hillel Director and I went up directly to speak with Dean Saffold, who was watching from her post a flight above us. She told us she would call in the SF Police. But the police could do nothing more than surround the Jewish students and community members who were now trapped in a corner of the plaza, grouped under the flags of Israel while an angry, out-of-control mob, literally chanting for our deaths, surrounded us. Dr. Astren and I went to stand with our students. This was neither free speech nor discourse, but raw physical assault.

Was I afraid? No, really more sad that I could not protect my students. Not one administrator came to stand with us. I knew that if a crowd of Palestinian or Black students had been there, surrounded by a crowd of white racists screaming racist threats, shielded by police, the faculty and staff would have no trouble deciding which side to stand on.

There was no safe way out of the Plaza. We had to be marched back to the Hillel House under armed SF police guard, and we had to have police guards remain outside

Hillel. I was very proud of the students, who did not flinch and who did not, even one time, resort to violence or anger in retaliation. Several community members who were swept up in the situation simply could not believe what they saw. One young student told me, "I have read about anti-Semitism in books, but this is the first time I have seen real anti-Semites, people who just hate me without knowing me, just because I am a Jew." She lives in the dorms. Her mother called and urged her to transfer to a safer campus.

Today is advising day. For me, the question is an open one: What do I advise the Jewish students to do?" – Laurie Zoloth, Director, Jewish Studies Program SFSU Campus.

Christians around the world must take seriously our God-appointed place in history as the protectors of the "Seed of Abraham." We cannot and we must not sit idly by as so many did in the 1930's and the 1940's while our Jewish brothers and sisters are facing such hatred, humiliation and even death!

Are you willing to take such a stand in support of our Jewish brothers and sisters and for the state of Israel? The time is coming quickly now when that question must be answered even right here in America. How will you answer?

Chapter Twenty

Ezra's Part in the "Final Return"

"Instead of their shame my people will receive a double portion, and instead of disgrace they will rejoice in their inheritance; and so they will inherit a double portion in their land [Israel] and everlasting joy will be theirs."
Isaiah 61:7

I can only hope that the time we have spent together walking through the pages of this book have in some way been helpful for us all to learn that the return of the Jews to the land of Israel is truly God's plan.

Nearly every prophet of the Old Testament wrote of this worldwide, end-time prophetic event over twenty-seven hundred years ago, and now those prophecies are being fulfilled. What exciting days we are blessed to be living in!

Every person who is part of the Ezra International team around the world is extremely honored to have even a small part in the return of the Jews of the Diaspora to their homeland. I have been laboring with this ministry for over nine years, and I can tell you that I have not met the first person who is associated with Ezra International who was looking for a "job" when they became a part of the team.

Each one of them has been called by God to this high calling, and they know it. It is with that deep sense of conviction that each one goes about their daily duties among the Jewish people with great joy and with a sense of accomplishment, of personally being used by God to fulfill Bible prophecy. Once again may I say they are just ordinary people, doing extraordinary things!

Many times the work they do is terribly difficult, with many frustrations. The weather conditions they work in are many times extremely harsh, especially in the Siberia region of Russia. They constantly have to struggle with political red-tape. We have a saying within Ezra, "It was easier for Moses to part the Red Sea than it is for the Ezra International staff to part the red-tape." But praise God, He always makes a way where there seems to be no way.

Perhaps you have picked up on a great truth during your reading. The truth of the matter is that the *aliyah* is far too big for any one individual or any one ministry to do it alone. That is why it is so very important for all of the organizations that have a love for Israel, the Jewish people and the *aliyah* to work hand in hand in this most holy work.

I think that King David said it best when he wrote these words in Psalm 133:1-3:

"Behold, how good and how pleasant it is for brethren to dwell together in unity! It is like the precious ointment upon the head, that ran down upon the beard, even Aaron's beard: that went down to the skirts of his garments: as the dew of Hermon, and as the dew that descended upon the mountains of Zion; for there the Lord commanded the blessing, even life for evermore."

It has been such a personal blessing for me to witness first-hand these many years how wonderfully well so many of the organizations laboring in the *aliyah* have worked together for one common goal. That goal, of course, is assisting God's chosen people to return to the land of their inheritance.

Ezra International has had a very close working relationship over the years with Bridges For Peace, The International Christian Embassy Jerusalem, Ministry to Israel, Ebenezer Emergency Fund (Operation Exodus), Good News Travel, Aliyah Highways, and of course with the many Jewish Agencies located in the various countries we are laboring in. Without this wonderful cooperation among the various organizations none of us would have been able to accomplish everything that has been done thus far.

So now the question remains to be answered, "What is Ezra International's part in this "Final Return?" We have already discussed a few of the responsibilities of Ezra in earlier chapters, but it is always good to have a bit of review as we share some additional information.

The Ezra International staff in the fourteen countries we are working in begins by making contact with the Jewish community. This is usually done through the Jewish Agency which the Jewish people are registered with in each city. It is this important agency that gives our workers the names and the addresses of their people so we can make the initial contact.

Other times we learn of their names through the many concerts and gatherings we provide for the Jewish community. Still other Jewish people are referred to us by family members or friends that we have assisted in the past. And often times the Israeli Embassy gives the people Ezra's contact information which enables them to receive the much needed financial assistance that is available through our ministry.

There is never a shortage of Jewish people to assist in their *aliyah*. A very large percentage of them sincerely want to leave for a better life in Israel where they can give their children a much better future.

During the initial contact, an in-depth consultation is done to determine the particular needs of each person or family and to determine to what extent the assistance that is needed will be.

If we locate individuals and families who are in need of food, clothing, medical equipment, medicines, etc., those immediate needs are cared for first. It is so vital to get their everyday living situations stabilized before moving onto the next phase of their preparation for their *aliyah.*

Just as quickly as we can get their daily lives in order, we proceed to the documentation phase of their preparation for departure.

The first hurdle that must be cleared is for each family member to acquire an international passport. In most of the former Soviet Union countries the cost for the passport is approximately forty-five dollars. So many of the people we assist are so poor they are having trouble putting a loaf of bread on the evening dinner table. Without the financial assistance of Ezra International these precious people would be unable to clear even the first hurdle of obtaining their passports.

Prior to passports being issued to each family member, the public records are checked very carefully by the government. If it is determined that a family owes any debt to the government they are denied their passport until the debt is cleared. These debts can be such things as unpaid rent on their government-owned apartment or perhaps an unpaid electric, water or gas bill. No matter what that debt may be, these Jewish people are stranded and unable to leave for Israel.

Prior to the walls of Communism coming down in 1991, it was "walls" that held them in; now it is "poverty." Ezra International is determined as God is determined that not one Jew is going to be left behind because of finances! Many times our second order of business is to pay off that government-owed debt, making it possible for the family to receive their passports.

After these first two hurdles are cleared and everyone has their passports, it is time for the family or individual to make their way to the Israeli Embassy located in the capital city of the country in which they are presently living.

The reason for the trip to the Embassy is for the required consultation they must go through to prove without a shadow of a doubt that they are Jewish before they are given their Israeli visas. It is necessary for each family member to attend these consultations, not just the head of the family. It is also necessary for them to bring documents to be used to prove they are Jews. These documents can be birth certificates, marriage licenses from the synagogue signed by a rabbi, a death certificate of a grandmother as well as several other possibilities.

It is not unusual for these individuals and families to make several trips to the embassy because they did not have sufficient documents to prove their "Jewishness." While traveling in Moldova our representative of that country took me to visit a family they had been working with for well over a year. This family had made fourteen such trips to the embassy, and it wasn't until the fifteenth trip that they were awarded their Israeli visas.

Everyone of these trips to the embassy can mean overnight train tickets for the entire family, overnight lodging, meals, taxis, buses, notary fees, etc., etc. Now if these people cannot afford a loaf of bread, how can they afford all of these expenses? Of course the answer is, they can't. Here again, this is where Ezra International steps into the picture. Ezra pays all of these travel expenses regardless of how many times the people must travel to the embassy.

Another very serious issue arises many times during the document process. We find many Jewish people whose documents were destroyed in World War II, perhaps they were destroyed in a fire, a flood, stolen or just lost. Many months and sometimes several years can be required to reestablish their documents to prove that they are Jews.

For one such family it took the Ezra staff in Kiev more than four years to get the necessary documents re-established in order for them to receive their Israeli visas.

We thank God for Tiesa who is a very important part of the office team in the Kiev office. Tiesa is in charge of assisting the Jewish people with their documents. She is seventy-two years old. She has recently had a serious bout with cancer, and still she has the energy of a twenty-year-old and the tenacity of a bulldog. Just as it is Ezra's desire that not one Jew be left behind because of finances, Tiesa is determined that not one person will be left behind because of lack of documents. Tiesa is such an encouragement to all who know her.

The average cost of bringing a person to the point of having their passport in hand, acquiring their visa, paying off any debts that are owed to the government, and paying for all of their travel expenses related to acquiring their visas, is approximately three hundred sixty dollars. These expenses are all cared for by the ministry of Ezra International with funds provided by our one-time givers, our monthly partners, and the other organizations that partner with Ezra International.

Once everything is in order, it is time to schedule their transportation to the nearest International airport. It is at this point that the cooperation of the other *aliyah* ministries comes into play. In the past, we contacted Good News Travel, who has operated over-the-road buses for the purpose of transporting the Olim (Jewish immigrants) to the port of Odessa to go to Israel by ship or to the closest international airport to board their flight to Tel Aviv. Today we work very closely with Aliyah Highways located in Kiev, Ukraine, which handles the same transportation services.

Not only is Ezra International deeply involved in assisting the Jewish people of fourteen countries in their return to Israel, but they are very much involved in assisting them with humanitarian aid before and after they leave.

Since Ezra's beginning in 1995, they have provided tons of humanitarian aid to 88 hospitals, 67 charitable organizations, 44 shelters, 17 prisons and 5 rehabilitation centers. Ezra also has feeding programs for Jews in Omsk, Siberia, and the Mountain Jews of Azerbaijan. They are operating feeding programs for street children in Kiev, Ukraine, and Omsk, Siberia.

Ezra International is also partnering with other organizations to provide a children's shelter in Kiev as well as co-sponsoring a beautiful orphanage in Kiev called "Father's House." It is estimated that there are over five thousand children living on the streets of Kiev alone. God has called Ezra International to save as many of them as possible.

One of the other important areas of work being done by Ezra International is educating the Body of Christ about what God is doing prophetically with Israel and the Jewish people in these last days.

This is accomplished by qualified Ezra speakers going throughout the world speaking in churches, appearing as exhibitors at denominational and other Christian conferences, doing television and radio appearances as well as speaking in home groups, Bible study groups, and civic organizations.

If you are a pastor, please let me encourage you to contact me at the Ezra International office by way of a phone call or an e-mail. Would you please prayerfully consider having me or one of the other qualified Ezra speakers come to your church for a service to share this end-time prophetic ministry with your congregation? I can assure you that your people will be greatly blessed as this new revelation is revealed to them and they are given an opportunity to be a blessing to the "Apple of God's eye" and the land of Israel.

I would like to encourage each of our readers to visit our web site at www.ezrausa.org to see a complete overview of all the areas of ministry that Ezra is involved in. You can also view a thirty minute video that is presently airing across the country on satellite television.

So, that is pretty much Ezra International's part in Israel's "Final Return." But what about *your* part in this end-time prophetic event? Do you have a part? Or is God just calling a chosen few to be involved in the re-gathering of the Jews to the land of Israel? Let's take a look at these questions together, shall we?

Chapter Twenty-One

And Now ... It's "Your Turn"

This is what the Sovereign Lord says:
"See, I will beckon to the Gentiles, I will lift up my banner
to the peoples; they [Gentiles] *will bring your sons in their*
arms and carry your daughters on their shoulders."
Isaiah 49:22

Well dear friends, as one of my former District Superintendents always liked to say, "This is where the rubber hits the road."

I have done my very best through the pages of this book to help all of us who are counted in the Body of Christ to see that we are living in a very important prophetic season of human history. It is extremely exciting to see Bible prophecy being fulfilled before our very eyes, but it is even more exciting to be a part of it. And now, God is giving *you* the opportunity to partner with Him in the re-gathering of His chosen people from the nations.

When we read the morning newspapers as it pertains to Israel, the former Soviet Union countries, anti-Semitism, Jews returning to their covenant land in huge numbers, the changing weather patterns, natural disasters, fanatical Islam, wars and rumors of wars, and so much more, it is like reading pages from God's own play book—the Word of God.

God has shown us very clearly through the Scriptures and through the prophets that it is His desire—in fact it is His eternal plan—for the Jews of the Diaspora to return to the Jewish state of Israel just prior to the return of Messiah.

It only seems natural for any of us who love God with all of our heart, mind, soul and strength and who have a desire to see His perfect will be fulfilled, to ask ourselves, "How can I be used by God to do my part in the re-gathering of His chosen people from the nations and to bring them back home from out of the Diaspora?

Do you recall our conversation in an earlier chapter concerning the deep love that God has put into the hearts of millions of Christian believers around the world for the Jewish people? I mentioned that man was incapable of putting that love into your heart. It was placed there by the Holy Spirit, and He didn't give you that love for the Jewish people just for the sake of doing it. He has done it for such a time as this.

The time that is remaining to rescue, return and restore the Jews of the Diaspora is very short. That window of opportunity is about to close on our Jewish friends of the former Soviet Union countries. As I said before, "time" is their greatest enemy.

It would have been utterly impossible for the more than one and a half million Jews who have already returned to Israel since the walls of Communism fell, to have made it home without the prayers, the physical labor and the financial assistance that has been given by people of the Body of Christ.

Perhaps you are already one of those people. If you are, may I say on behalf of the sixty-five thousand Jewish people that Ezra International has assisted in their return, thank you so very much for your kindness, your love for them and for your willingness to be a partner with God in this most Holy Work. I know without any doubt whatsoever that your life has already been richly blessed as you have blessed His people and His land.

Remember what Genesis 12:3 promises us? *"I will bless those who bless you and those who curse you I will curse."*

For those of you who have said to God, "Here am I, use me," I want you to remember that not only have you been a blessing to the Apple of God's eye, but you have also impacted nations in a huge way in the process. You have impacted both Israel and also the nations that the Jews have escaped from. What you have already done and what you are continuing to do has already been recorded in the archives of Heaven!

So once again, I must ask the simple yet most important question: "Is this high calling of being a part of the *aliyah* limited to a chosen few or has God ordained that the entire Body of Christ is to be involved in it?"

I feel that God has answered this question very well, leaving no doubt in our minds that it is His intension for the entire Body of Christ to be involved in this "Final Return" of the Jewish people to the state of Israel. Let's look at Isaiah 49:22 one more time for the answer.

This is what the sovereign Lord says, "See, I will beckon to the Gentiles, I will raise up my banner to the peoples; and they [the Gentiles] *will carry your sons in their arms and your daughters on their shoulders"* (emphasis mine).

I may be of a simple mind, but I just cannot see how it could be any plainer that it is God's intension for the entire Body of Christ to be involved in partnering with Him in the rebuilding of "physical Israel" as well as "Spiritual Israel." Such an honor and such a privilege He is giving us.

Does this mean that the Body of Christ is to lay aside the many other callings that God has placed on the Church and its people? Such important callings as feeding the hungry, clothing the naked, visiting the sick, caring for the widows, winning the lost, healing the broken-hearted, physical healings and deliverance. Is the Church being asked to stop opening Christian schools, building new church buildings, starting new churches around the world, sending out missionaries into the nations with the Good News of the Gospel? Absolutely not!

Every one of these callings is essential for the Church to be involved in as well as many others. I am simply suggesting that within the past sixteen-plus years since the fall of Communism, God has placed one more very important calling on the Body of Christ that has been overlooked by so many. Yes, time is short, but we still have time to pick up the torch that God is calling us to carry in these last days.

We must understand that this calling which God has placed on the Body of Christ to be involved in the *aliyah*, assisting the Jews of the Diaspora in their return to the state of Israel, is no less of a calling than the many others God has given to the Church.

The Church has done a wonderful job over the centuries of responding to and carrying out all of the other callings of God that were just mentioned and many more besides. None of us will fully realize the extent of the effect the Church and each of our lives have had on the world in general and individual lives in particular until we are ushered into the very presence of God.

Time and space does not permit the listing of all the many wonderful blessings that have been brought into this world by the Church of Jesus Christ. The hospitals and the medical clinics started in some of the most remote areas of the planet, the schools, colleges, universities, humanitarian aid centers, just to mention a very few.

The Church has impacted this world as nothing else has, but our work is not yet finished. There is still much to do.

Many times when I am speaking in churches or while appearing on television I will mention the fact that much of the evangelical church is in what I call the "Rapture Mode."

In other words, so many in the church just want to put on their white "rapture robes," go to the top of "Rapture Mountain" and eat "Rapture Twinkies" until Messiah comes. As I am always quick to point out, that idea isn't even Biblical. Jesus said that we are to *occupy until He comes*. That sounds like work to me!

If these same people want to hasten the coming of Messiah, I instruct them to get involved in assisting the Jewish people to return to the state of Israel.

The time is now for the Church, the Body of Christ, to stand up and be counted. It is time for us all to say, "Here am I, Lord, use me." Time is quickly running out.

So, may I ask each of you this question? What about you? Have you come to the place that you are willing to be used by Abba to help bring His children home in their "Final Return?"

I am reminded of a very frightening event that I experienced about four years ago. When Linda and I are not traveling, we have been blessed to care for our two youngest grandchildren, Austin and Aidan, while our son and our daughter-in-law are working at Universal Studios in Orlando.

One afternoon when Austin was about three years old and just at the age where he was able to open doors, I was passing through our livingroom when I spotted the front door standing wide open. I must tell you that when I saw that open door my heart dropped into my shoes. I knew immediately that it was Austin who had opened the door and he had quickly disappeared.

I remember running out onto the front porch and calling his name, "Austin, Austin where are you?" When there was no response I shot across the front lawn and onto the sidewalk, still calling out his name. I looked up the street only to see a deserted street. I turned and looked down the street. It was then that I spotted my "Prodigal Grandson" toddling away in the opposite direction. I remember crying out to God in my spirit, "Thank you God, Thank you God!"

After sprinting down the sidewalk and capturing our little "runaway" I quickly returned him to the house, handed him to Linda, dashed as fast as I could legally drive to the Home Depot, and purchased a childproof lock to install on my front door at a level unreachable by a wondering three-year-old.

It wasn't long after I had installed the new lock that I received a vision from God. In this vision I saw the very same plot play out with little Austin leaving the house on his own. But this time there was a bit of a twist in the story. This time, when I ran onto the sidewalk—looking first to the left and then to the right—there was no Austin to be seen.

In a panic I began to comb the neighborhood looking for our little guy but finding nothing. Linda came out, and joined in the search, but still no Austin to be found anywhere. We phoned the police who came quickly and assisted in the search. We pounded on several of our neighbor's doors and begged them to help us find and return our little grandson home to us.

By now, several hours had passed, and our hearts and our spirits had hit rock bottom. With so many abductions of small children taking place around the country, you can just imagine what must have been going through our minds.

It was just about dusk when we returned to the sidewalk in front of our own home. Still in a panic, I remember thanking everyone who had assisted us in the search for little Austin.

I remember in this vision, it was then that I turned, looking down the street and seeing through the dimming light of day the most beautiful sight I had ever witnessed in my entire life. Walking toward me, Linda, and our wonderful neighbors was a complete stranger carrying so tenderly in his arms the little lost love of our lives. I ran down the street as fast as I could run to meet them. He said to me, "Does this little guy belong to you?" Taking Austin in my arms, with tears streaming down my face I said, "Oh yes, this is my little grandson who has been lost most of the day, and now you have brought him home to us. How can I ever repay you for your kindness and for your concern?" This stranger—someone I didn't even know—was a real hero to me and my family because he had brought our precious little grandson home.

This wonderful stranger would always have a special place in our hearts, he would always be welcome in our home, and he would always have a place at our table. There would never be enough that I could possibly do for him in thanks for what he had done for us by bringing our Austin home.

After the vision had ended, I began thinking about what God had just allowed me to see. I remember so clearly as the lesson of this vision struck my spirit I began to weep and sob.

I knew that God allowed me to see by way of this personal event exactly how He feels every time one of His precious children is brought home to Him and how He must feel toward the one who brought His child home.

The events of this vision God allowed me to experience that day are carried out everyday of every week of every month as the Body of Christ is making it possible for the staff and workers of Ezra International and other Christian organizations to carry His precious children back to their home.

You can be certain that God has a very special place in His heart for those individuals, churches and organizations who love enough, who care enough, and who want to bless His children by helping them return home.

If you are one of those people, once again I want to thank you from the bottom of my heart for what you are doing for our Jewish brothers and sisters.

If you have not become involved in what God is doing with His people by returning them to their "Promised Land" but you want to be used of God, I have good news—no, I have great news for you! This calling I have been speaking about is not for a "chosen few," it is for who-so-ever-will, and that my dear friend includes you!

By now you may be asking, "What must I do to be used by God in the return of His people to their own land? I want to be a blessing to His people and help save as many of them while there is still time, but I don't know how."

I can tell you that what you must do to bless His people is not that difficult at all.

If you are truly sincere about this call on your life, the first thing that must happen is for you to approach the throne of God with a repentant heart and repent of any anti-Semitic things you may have done or you may have spoken in the past. It is very possible for all of us to have engaged in such activities somewhere in our past without even being aware of it. I'm certain that you probably feel as I do. I would rather repent of something I'm not guilty of rather than not repent of something known—or even unknown—that needs repenting of. It is always good to enter into a new day or a new calling with a perfectly clean slate.

May I ask you to pray this simple prayer of repentance as it pertains to our Jewish friends? Let's pray.

"Heavenly Father, I come to You today with a heart of true repentance. Father, please forgive me of anything in my past or in the present that is or even looks or sounds like anti-Semitic behavior or speech. I realize now more than ever before, that the Jewish people are still the "Apple of Your eye." I realize today that I owe my salvation to the Jewish people because our Savior and Lord came through the lineage of David. The Jewish people gave us the prophets, the apostles and the precious Word of God and so much more. Now, as they have blessed me so richly, I want to be a blessing to

*them in return. Father, I have not experienced that deep love
in my heart for the Jewish people that You and millions of
Christians around the world have for them but I sincerely
want to. Will You please fill my heart to overflowing with
that same love for Your people and the land of Israel? By
faith I receive it now and I thank You from the bottom of
my heart. I want to stand with Your people in their desperate
time of need. I was not even born during the days of the
horrors of the Holocaust but I am here now and with Your
help Abba, I will not be silent any longer. I will stand for
and stand with the state of Israel and Your Chosen People
by praying for them and praying for the peace of Jerusalem
daily and by doing everything I can do with Your help to
assist them in their return to their own land." Amen*

If I know anything about God, I know without any
doubt that the prayer you just prayed has touched the very
heart of Abba. Now you are prepared to take the next step
in your stand with the land of Israel and the Jewish people.

It is so important for you to become connected with
a Christian organization that is blessing Israel by laboring
in the *aliyah*, rescuing, returning and restoring the Jewish
people to their own land.

I have said this before, but I will say it again just so
there will be no misunderstanding. The Ezra International
board, the staff and volunteers around the world, would
be most honored if you would become involved with us
through your prayers and by becoming a financial partner.
As was mentioned in an earlier chapter, Ezra International
has already assisted over sixty-five thousand Jews to make
their *aliyah*, and we are presently assisting over thirty-one
thousand more. Obviously your prayers and your financial
gifts are desperately needed by Ezra; however, it is far more
important to me for you to get connected somewhere if
you do not feel led by the Holy Spirit to partner with this
organization. As I said before, "We don't care who brings

these precious people home; let's just get them home!" So please, get connected somewhere!

Here is another opportunity you may wish to consider. On regular occasions I personally take volunteers with me to Kiev, Ukraine, for a ten-day, hands-on Jeremiah 16:16 "fishing trip." On this trip you will have the opportunity to visit the Jewish families that Ezra International is working with and preparing them to make their *aliyah*. You will personally carry humanitarian aid into their homes to sustain them until their departure for Israel.

You will board a Ukrainian train for the overnight trip to Odessa, located on the Black Sea, where we will meet with Galena, Ezra's representative for that region of the country. Again, you will visit many more Jewish families as well as visits to historical sites from WWII where thousands of Jews were massacred by the Nazis.

Scheduled into the ten-day itinerary are visits to "Father's House," the beautiful orphanage that Ezra International co-sponsors with other organizations. You will also visit the children's shelter that is operated by Ezra for street children. You will participate in Ezra's feeding program for street children of Kiev.

You will be a guest at the Ezra International's office in Kiev and meet the entire staff and so much more. If you would like more information about this volunteer opportunity you need only to contact me personally at the U.S.A. Ezra office. The contact information can be found on the last page of this book.

At this time, Ezra is in the process of setting up a network of representatives in every state in the U.S. to take the message of *aliyah* to the Body of Christ. We are looking for men and women who have a desire to educate the church about what God is doing prophetically with Israel and the Jewish people in their "Final Return" and to assist in the fund raising process. After a time of prayer, seeking the Lord's leading for your life, should you feel that this would be an area of ministry that God would have you serve in please contact me for an application form.

And finally, one of the most important ways you can partner with God in His children's return to Eretz Israel is by giving of your financial resources. May we never forget the words of the Apostle Paul as he wrote to the church in Rome:

For if the Gentiles [that's us] *have shared in the Jews' spiritual blessings, they* [Gentiles] *owe it to the Jews to share with them their material blessings"* (Romans 15:27b emphasis mine).

God said to Abram in Genesis 12:3b: *"And all peoples on earth will be blessed through you."*

That Scripture has come to pass for more than four thousand years as Jewish people the world over have blessed the nations, and now God is calling us to be a blessing to them in their struggles to return to the land of their inheritance.

I always remind congregations, conference attendees, television viewers, and radio listeners wherever I speak that no financial gift to the work of Ezra International is too large or too small.

One of our wonderful monthly partners is an elderly lady from the state of Texas who for several years has sent so faithfully her five dollar cash gift to Ezra International. I know that her humble gift to bless the children of God is as important in God's eyes as that gift of ten or twenty thousand dollars that may come from other sources. I always think of the widow's mite when I see her gift arrive at the Ezra office.

Please allow me to encourage you to become a monthly partner with Ezra International by giving whatever the Holy Spirit should lay on your heart to give. You may give your first gift by making your check payable to Ezra International and mailing it to the address found on the last page of this book.

With each monthly gift you send, you will receive a tax receipt letter with a return envelope to be used for your next month's gift. All gifts to Ezra are tax deductible as allowed by law.

And now may the words of the Prophet Isaiah ring ever true in our hearts, our mind and our spirits:

"For Zion's sake I will not keep silent, for Jerusalem's sake I will not remain quiet, till her righteousness shines out like the dawn, her salvation like a blazing torch. I have posted watchmen on your walls, O Jerusalem; they will never be silent day or night. You who call on the Lord, give yourselves no rest, and give Him no rest till He establishes Jerusalem and makes her the praise of the earth" (Isaiah 62:1, 6-7 KJV)

I leave you now with this prayer found in Numbers 6:22-27:

The Lord said to Moses, "Tell Aaron and his sons, this is how you are to bless the Israelites. Say to them: 'The Lord bless you and keep you; the Lord make His face shine upon you and be gracious to you; the Lord turn His face toward you and give you peace.' So they will put my name on the Israelites, and I will bless them."